HOOD DRIVEN II

Last Breed of Gangsta's
A Crime Novel
By D Mack

D MACK

Facebook: Hood Driven

Twitter: @HoodDriven

Instagram: @hooddrivenbook

Deep-Street Publications
Detroit, MI 48227

Copyright © 2008, revised 2021

ISBN 978-0-615-43767-5
Cover Design: Eric Thomas of Mysic Essence & revised by William C.

Printed In the United States of America

PLEASE DO NOT ATTEMPT
ANY OF THE THINGS DEPICTED
WITHIN THIS STORY... THIS IS FOR
ENTERTAINMENT PURPOSES ONLY.

By no means do I glorify violence. I just touch
on reality the way it was revealed to me and
so many others like me. It is what it is.

Nothing can be Everything....
Everything can be Nothing....

Chinese Philosophy

In everyone of us there's an untapped force that's waiting to be awakened. And once it's awoke, its not always up to the individual as to which direction the energy will go. We may find ourselves driven to places of constant uncertainty, dark thoughts and false hope, while we strive to find ourselves in places where the sun always shines, and the grass is always green. In turn, every hood across the globe has an elite group of individuals who are willing to rise to the occasion to reverse the ill-effects of a double-edged circumstance and win... Although the concept of winning seems to be decayed in a shallow grave. "Last Breed of Gangsta's" is the sequel to the spellbounding Hood Driven series. They say one can run but he can't hide. And in this alphabet of life, the obstacles sometimes come before, but mostly after the "G." Then, when the sirens blare like they so frequently do, who gets the last laugh?

"Come on, walk a little faster baby, we almost there! Now when we get to this next stop, rest your hands behind ya' back as if you're handcuffed, and don't say nothing."

As they approached the tall razor-trimmed gate, the heavyset white officer at the control booth glanced through the tinted bullet proof glass, then pressed the speaker button on the large square switchboard.

"State your name, rank, your inmate's number, and purpose of transport."

"Co. Robinson, rank 1st Lt. Inmate's number is 617323. Departing from building A-block to building D-block for a level 4 disruption."

The officer stood up from his seat and stepped a little closer to the window before responding.

"Couldn't it wait 'til the A.M for the transport cowboy?"

"That's a negative due to the fact that the segregation unit is packed with members of this inmate's rivals. And you know as well as I do, we don't take life threatening situations lightly. Now like I said before, this is a level 4 situation."

The big bellied white officer glanced out the window again. He focused on the inmate for a moment, then on the officer, then back to the inmate. He scratched the side of his huge head in a puzzled manner, then picked up the phone and attempted to dial a number. But just as quickly, decided to ask a few more questions before he made the call.

"How did it start and who was involved?"

"Hmff." The first Lt. released an irritable sigh before giving a response.

"First of all, I hope you don't expect me to name every individual involved, cause it's too damn many. Second of all, you're takin' me back to the days of dealin' with rookie's, cause only rookie's ask shit like that. But if you just gotta' know in more detail, it was mostly the mo'bites involved. And it started because of a religious group demonstration."

The inquisitive officer stared blankly with the phone in his hand for about fifteen seconds, then reluctantly hung up and opened the gate with the press of a button.

The walk through the several gates was long and intense, but the moment Ray Ray and Sheila made it to the car, Ray Ray immediately changed out of the correctional officer uniform into a Rocawear track suit, while Sheila changed out of the blue prison uniform into Burberry jeans with the matching shirt. She glanced back at the maximum security prison as they pulled off in a hurry and threw up her middle finger with strong emphasis. Ray Ray smiled at her actions and replied. "I feel ya baby, fuck'em." Sheila was super excited and could barely gather herself.

"Oh my God! I can't believe you just broke me out. Please God tell me I'm not dreamin, tell me it's real."

Sheila leaned toward him and rubbed his face with tears of joy in her eyes. She spoke in a trembling voice, with tears now streaming down her face. "Baby those two years felt like twenty without you. I missed you sooo much."

"I know baby, cause I missed you too. But I gotchu now baby... I gotchu."

After 45 minutes of driving, Sheila felt a sense of relief when she saw the sign that read, 'Leaving Coldwater Mighigan, entering Detroit. She hated the redneck town that she'd been incarcerated in and vowed to never step foot in it again unless she was a politician that came to change their racist policies for the better or came with the intentions of Timothy McVeigh.

They arrived at a safe house on the westside of Detroit that Ray Ray purchased for this occasion, and the first thing Sheila did was scan each room expecting to see her daughters.

"Ray Ray, where's Myonly and Love?" She asked anxiously as she continued to look through the house.

"Baby they in L.A with Smoke right now. I didn't wanna bring'em on this mission cause shit coulda' got ugly. So just hold tight bae, we leavin the first thing in the morning, okay?"

Sheila displayed a slight sign of disappointment, but quickly shook it off as the thought of their A.M departure set in. She walked up to Ray Ray and slipped into his arms in a warm embrace, then softly whispered. "I don't ever wanna go back to that place Ray Ray, never."

Ray Ray's reply came in the form of a soft kiss on her lips.

She immediately melted into the kiss, offering her tongue with a slight urgency. Their tongues eagerly swirled across one another as they both held a tight grip. Ray Ray's hands methodically began to slide across

Sheila's body, taking in the softness and warmness of her every curve. He gripped her plump butt with both hands, pulling her body tight against his so she could feel his erection through his pants. Sheila slid her legs apart and pressed herself against him and began to grind in a slow circular motion. She loved the way his hardness felt pressed up against her sex. He unfastened her pants and slid his hand down her panties. His fingers were instantly soaked as he worked them inside her wetness. A few moments later, Sheila's moaning became louder, and she suddenly dropped to her knees as she came.

Ray Ray burst out laughin as she sat there on the floor breathing heavy from the sudden orgasm.

"Damn baby, you really haven't been gettin none, have you?"

That's not funny Ray Ray, and no, I haven't been gettin none."

"Baby I thought you might've got yo'self a girlfriend, I would'na held it against you. It's a little more acceptable when it's two women involved." Sheila looked up with a sarcastic expression before responding.

"Well I don't care what 'spose to be more acceptable, you know I don't get down like that. And speakin of gettin' some, what about you, have you been gettin' some since I been gone, huh?"

Ray Ray casually bent down and scooped Sheila's body up in his arms before replying.

"As a matter of fact, I have been gettin' some. Every time I jacked this dick off thinkin' about you. Now let me take you in here and show you how much I been missin' you. And nomore premature ejaculations, a'ight?"

Sheila smiled and giggled as he carried her into the bedroom....

The light was off and the room was illuminated by candlelight only as Ray Ray laid her on the bed. Sheila marveled at the way he had the room decorated for their special night, and suddenly had an overwhelming feeling of admiration for her lover and best friend. The scented candles filled her nostrils and gave an inviting feel to the atmosphere. And the grapes, wine, strawberries, and whip cream, gave an even greater feeling of invitation. Sheila's loins begged to be pleased, and her mind roamed as her heart began to thump rapidly in her chest. The soft music by Jill Scott entitled *"Comes to the light"* brought a peaceful harmony and an aura of tranquility with it... Not to mention the two-hundred various-colored roses that covered the entire bed, it blew Sheila away... Tears of happiness flowed down her beautiful face, and all she could do was melt when she felt Ray Ray's wet kisses. He started from her neck, then made his way around to her soft tities. And it wasn't long before her breathing began to grow heavy again, while her anxious hands reached out for him. Ray waisted no time lickin and suckin on her stiff brown nipples, workin his way down to her chiseled stomach. He was truly diggin their foreplay thang, but he felt that his bride had waited long enough for this. His lustful kisses were now centered on her sweet pussy, and the more he licked and sucked, the harder her body would quiver. He toyed with her clitoris with his flickering tongue, then sucked down hard as if he was trying to retrieve it from her body.

"Oooohh! Bay-bee damn. Oow shit! Ray Ray!" Sheila panted and moaned as she arched her back, attempting to slightly withdraw from the overwhelming pleasure... But as she squirmed and wiggled, it was too no avail, 'cause Ray Ray wasn't about to let-up... He continued to eat her til he tasted more of her juices, then casually removed his boxers... He climbed between her thick brown thighs, eagerly pushing his throbbing dick in her tight-gripping pussy. His movements inside her wetness were long, steady strokes. And she eagerly opened her legs even wider to allow him more access to her aching hole.

"Ahhh, yes baby! Oow!" Sheila cried out when she felt his thrust start to speed up... She locked her legs around his waist, and unconsciously dug her nails in his lower back... Ray Ray went deeper now, and the more he thought about how much he missed his lady, the freakier he would get.

"You miss me mama? Huh! You missed this good dick didn't you!" Ray Ray talked enticingly outloud while rotating his hips in a circular motion. His hard flesh twirled around inside her, touching spots that she'd forgot was there. He traced her nipples with his tongue, then gripped her ass for leverage to accomodate his thrust... Sheila was truly on fire at this point, and she gyrated her hips to match his rhythm. Her tities bounced freely as her fuck-faces changed. And the more he watched her, the harder he would pound.

"Oow shit Sheila, I missed my hot pussy... I missed my hot pussy like crazy baby." ... Ray Ray steady talked as he continued to pound.

"Keep them legs open just like that. Let me dig it out. You still like it like that, don't you? ... Let me fuck it hard."

Ray Ray's freak-talk drove Sheila crazy. And her hormones were officially hay-wire.

She slung her hips forward as Ray Ray pounded inside of her relentlessly, then closed her eyes tightly and whimpered through every pump.

Ray Ray pulled out momentarily, turning Sheila to the

side. He slapped her on the ass, then slid back up in it in a hurry.

"Ooh shit Ray Ray! Damn it feels so good baby! Yes baby, I missed you so mu- aaahggg! Sssmmm!"

Ray Ray admired his wife's beauty all over again as he held her cocked leg and banged it hard from the side.

He fucked her like a maniac in several more positions before they both ended up savagely fuckin on the floor.

As Ray Ray perspired and came close to bussin his load, he gripped her waist tight and pumped her fiercely from the back... Her ass shook better than jello and cushioned his balls as she took the aggressive thrashin posted on all fours... Ray Ray pumped his way to the ultimate sensation, but Sheila somehow knew she'd get there first.

"Ooh! Ooh! Oooooh! Ray Ray! Baby oh shit! Aaaaaaahhhhggggg! ...Ssssmmmmmm! Unnhhhgg!" The moment Sheila bussed, Ray Ray swiftly pulled his pole out and sprayed a heavy load of semen all over her tooted-up ass... They both smiled at one another as they attempted to regulate their heavy breathing. They relaxed for awhile, then spent the rest of the night monitoring the news between each sex-session... Wondering how long it would be before the escape was heavily broadcasted.

CHAPTER 2

The following morning, Sheila rolled her naked body over as Ray Ray placed the breakfast tray in front of her.

"Okay baby! Breakfast in bed, huh." She said excitedly.

"Yup! Now eat up so we can get up outta here."

Sheila smiled as she examined all the contents of the tray then blurted, "That betta' not be no pork on my tray."

"Girl shut up, don't come talkin' that pork prison shit to me. And fa' yo' information, that's Canadian turkey bacon, and if you don't want it, pass it over here."

Sheila slapped his hand back as he reached for her bacon.

"I thought so." said Ray Ray with a slight grin.

As Sheila sat their eating, Ray Ray couldn't help but to notice how extremely beautiful she was. She still had that same caramel brown skin, with her same long black hair that she wore in a ponytail. He was happy that she didn't cut it, cause it still dropped gracefully down the center of her back well past her petite ass. She sort'a resembled the actor Sally Richardson before Sally cut her hair.

He leaned over and kissed her for no apparent reason except the fact that he was glad to be reunited with his wife.

"Baby, why did you just kiss me while I'm sittin' over here with a mouth full of eggs?" Sheila asked with a smirk on her face.

Ray Ray pecked her on the lips again before responding.

"Cause you wifey and I can kiss them luscious thangs whenva' I feel like it, without a reason." he added matter-of-factly.

"Well since you put it like that, gimee some sugar now baby," she playfully pushed a mouthful of chewed up food to the front of her mouth.

"Ull girl you nasty." Squawked Ray Ray as he scooted away from her.

She playfully chased him trying to force a kiss on him as he ran around the room eluding her.

"Okay, okay baby, I swallowed it, look." She opened her empty mouth to let him see the food was gone, then tried to kiss him again but he suddenly stopped her and focused on her with a baffled expression.

"What's wrong baby, why you lookin at me like that?" She asked with concern in her voice. Ray Ray pulled her closer to inspect the thin scar that he'd just noticed over her left eye.

"How 'da fuck did that happen?" He asked in an angered tone.

Sheila looked toward the floor as the memory of the fight with another female inmate resurfaced, then answered.

"Baby, that's what comes with the territory. It's what happens in prison, so don't sweat it. And the one thing you should know is, I handled my business. You should see hers!" They both burst out laughin, then finished their breakfast.

Two hours later......

"You got everything baby?" asked Ray Ray as they prepared to leave.

"Yeah baby, let's go. I need to see my babies in a hurry."

He smiled as Sheila hurried past him to the door. She was hyped-up at the thought of seeing her children and being a free woman.

And during one of her and Ray Ray's rest periods between making love the night before, the only other subject she spoke about besides her children was Assata Shakur. She talked about how she had a newfound respect for Assata's exile situation to Cuba, because prison is a terrible place to be. And in her opinion, most of the people in prison didn't deserve to be there, because prison is just big business at the expense of inferior people.

Sheila suddenly froze in her tracks when she opened the door, and just as quickly, she slammed it shut. Ray Ray hastily asked, "What's wrong?" but before she could respond, he found the answer as he looked out the window and saw the blue and white Detroit police car parked out front. "Damn!" he squawked as he dropped his bags and ran towards the bedroom... Sheila heard him rambling around as she peeked out the window to observe the police closer.

A few moments later, she noticed Ray Ray abruptly spring into view headed for the front door with a tightly gripped fully automatic AR-15.

She swiftly jumped in front of him. "No No No baby wait!" He pushed her aside, then fidgeting opened the door. And just as he took aim, Sheila was right back in his space, locking her arms around his body as tight as she could, yelling frantically in his ear.

"No Ray Ray, look! They're not for us. Look!"

It was then that he saw the black Regal in front of the squad car, with three youngsta's stretched out with palms on the hood of the Regal.

When the scene fully registered, he quickly dipped

back in the door with Sheila undetected, leaving the police unaware of the fact that they were about to be swiss cheese... Ray Ray and Sheila stared at each other for a moment in silence as they both let their adrenaline settle, then he went to the bedroom and put the gun up.

When he returned, he looked at her with a silly expression and joked, "Let's get the fuck up outta' here before our paranoid asses tell on ourselves." Sheila burst out laughin' as she walked up and gave him a tight hug. And gazed at her man with a sincere look of admiration before they left. They made it to the interstate ten minutes later headed for the Detroit Metro Airport.

"OOW that's my jam," said Sheila as she turned the volume up on the radio. She rocked back-n-forth as Usher featuring Lil John and Ludacris blared through the speakers. *"Tell me again, can we be lovers and friends."* She sung the words and snapped her fingers as the green rented Dodge Intrepid floated down the interstate. Creating distance between themselves and the motor-city madness that she desperately wanted to leave behind.

"Ha Ha Ha, Uncle Smoke that's not fair," whined Myonly as she laughed at Smoke's homerun hit with the plastic baseball bat.

"I'm gon' do that every time if you don't pitch the ball harder than that babygirl."

"Get'em next time Myonly." Yelled her five-year-old sister Love as she stood at second base patting her glove as if she was ready for war. The game was tied at 5-5, and after the last outs, Smoke was up to bat again.

Myonly stood there in her pitchers stand with a slight

look of uncertainty. She hesitated before she pitched the ball. Her 7-year-old frame slightly vibrated from the nervousness she felt from the situation.

"Whussup babygirl?" yelled Smoke. "Pitch 'dat ball so I can knock it out the park and end this game." Smoke's wife Ebony smiled and sympathized with her.

"Don't be so hard on her baby, give her a break." Smoke gave a smile in return then answered.

"Why, so Ray Ray can kill me when he finds out."

Suddenly, Myonly ran over to her sister Love.

"Let's switch places Love, you pitch this time and let me play second base."

Love looked at her sister with a puzzled expression yet spoke with charisma in her young tone.

"Myonly, I know you are nervous, but you gon' be alright. You know I can't switch places with you, you know what daddy always say, *You can't change the game in the ninth inning,* so don't expect me too. Now go strike uncle Smoke out." Myonly slowly walked back to her position as her sister's words resonated in her head. She took a deep breath, then took one step forward.

She gave Smoke the eye of the tiger as she wined up the ball. Love and the other children steadily cheered her on.

"Get'em Myonly, get'em this time." Myonly's winding motion sped up, and just as the cocked ball was leaving her hand, Bomp! Bomp!

The horn from the shiny black 745 Beemer with 22-inch Giovonni rims caused her to slightly twitch. Seconds later, the ball was sent flying out of sight, which made it the last homerun of the game. Smoke looked over at the occupant of the car as he ran the bases.

"Yo' Smoke! Let me holla' atchu cuz." Myonly stared at the man as if she wanted to do him serious bodily harm.

Smoke scooped her up and placed her on his shoulders.

"You still a champ babygirl, cause you didn't give up, okay?" After she nodded her head yes, he put her down and walked over to the car.

"Whuddup playa," he greeted the man.

"Same fight different round cuz. I was on my way to see you, but when I was passin' through here, I thought I recognized you, so it saved me a trip. Anyway, I'm tryna get on, you straight?"

"Yeah, I'm straight, whatchu tryna cop?"

"Ten chicken's baby."

"A'ight," I'll get back atchu in about a hour loc."

"Fasho cuz." responded the man known as K-loke as he prepared to pull off.

Suddenly they both looked up as heavy base thumped and lyrics from the rapper, 'The Game' poured from the approaching candy red H2 Hummer.

The driver known as Damu cruised to a slow stop beside Smoke and K-loke. All four of the occupants in the H2 had grimacing facial expressions as they stared at Smoke and Kay. The sun glistened off Damu's jet black skin creating a shiny appearance to his long corn rows. After a few moments of silence amongst them, he cut the music down.

"Yo' Smoke, let me holla atchu blood." Smoke turned to Kay and told him he'd see him later at the agreed time.

"You want me to hold up a minute cuz? Cause you know dude think he 'da shit."

"Naw fam I'm straight, I'll get atcha later a'ight?"

"A'ight cuz, see you then." Damu and Kay traded mean stares as his black Beemer pulled off slow.

Smoke approached the driver's side window.

"Whuddup dawg, what's all that mean muggin' about?"

Damu instinctively scratched the side of his head before responding.

"Check this out blood, I specifically remember me tellin' you I didn't want you fuckin' wit' no crabs on that tip. I told you don't sell them niggas shit."

"Hold up dawg." Smoke cut him off. "First of all, who 'da fuck is you to specifically tell me anything. And second of all, I told you a long time ago that I don't get off into yall lil' crip and blood beefs. We don't get down like that in Detroit. Whoeva' got the paper for the work, that's who get 'da work, you dig?" Damu's nostrils flared open before he responded.

"Check this out blood, the first thing you gon' learn, is you ain't in Detroit nomoe. And despite how silly you may think our way of life is, it's still our way of life and the shit is still real. And yeah, some of my people got truces with a few of them crab sets, but I seriously doubt if we ever get a truce with them niggas. The blood that's been spilled between us runs too deep. Deep as in my baby brother, my first cousin, my bitch, and my ace, and vice versa, you dig? So, check this out blood, this my last time tellin' you not to sell them niggas no work, or you can get a up close and personal history lesson on the reality of bangin'."

Smoke ran his hand across his short brush waves like he always did when he became upset, then stepped closer to Damu and grimaced.

"You threatenin' me dawg? Huh?"

Damu held his same cold stare before replying.

"If you really knew anything about me, you'd know I don't make threats blood, I make promises." The Hummer suddenly skidded off before Smoke could respond.

"Yeah whateva' nigga!" Smoke yelled aloud as the Hummer floated up the street.

"Ebony, you and the kids go over mama's house for awhile and I'll swing through later okay. I got some business to handle."

Ebony displayed an irritated expression, and she never made eye contact with Smoke. She just called for Myonly and Love to get ready to go...

****

As Yvonne laid in bed next to her man Rob, she smiled to herself as she reflected back on the way they met.

"Hello," said Yvonne as she answered the ringing phone.

"May I speak to Quewhanna?"

"I'm sorry, you must have the wrong number cause nobody lives here by that name."

"Oh, I apologize Ms. bye." Click!

......Riiiiiing. "Hello."

"Is Quewhanna there?"

"I'm afraid not, because the only woman that lives here is me. And once again, my name is not Quewhanna."

"Aw naw, please forgive me, this is not a prank call or anything like that... It's just that my sister Quewhanna recently came out of a drug rehab center, and I was really anxious to talk to her. My mother gave me this number and I must've wrote it down wrong, so once again please forgive me."

"It's no problem-"

"Rob, my name is Rob. And yours is-?"

"Yvonne."

"Yvonne that's a very pretty name, and it's unique. Ya' know if you spell it backwards, it's pronounced Ennovy, which is a French word that means Silver Rose. Do you know anything about a silver rose Yvonne?"

"As a matter of fact, I don't?"

"Well silver roses are considered the most exotic roses on the face of the earth. They originated in New Zealand but can commonly be found in Paris."

"Impressive," answered Yvonne, even though she felt he made the whole thing up.

"Have you been to either of those places Rob?"

"Yup, and I gotta say, if you've never been, you definitely wanna put those places on your future vacation list because it's an experience that you'll never forget."

"I'll be sure to do that Rob."

"Are you from L.A, or did you relocate from somewhere else Yvonne?"

"Actually, I relocated here from Detroit."

"Is that right?"

"Yup."

"I can tell from your accent." Rob admitted.

"Is that good or bad?" asked Yvonne humorously.

"How could a voice like that be a bad thing Yvonne?"

"Well some people don't like the language of relocaters."

"Well I'm not some people, and if your appearance goes hand in hand with that voice, Tara Banks betta' watch out."

Yvonne bust out laughin' before she could reply.

"Oh no you didn't go to the model incenuation."

"Maybe I did, why? Don't you think you're pretty enough to be a model?"

"Well, it's like this, I'm not the kind of woman who suffers from low self esteem, but modeling is definitely out of the question."

"How tall are you Yvonne?"

"I'm 5'9."

"How much do you weigh?"

"Not a lot, but I could stand to lose a few pounds."

"Well it ain't a woman on the planet who don't think

she could stand to lose weight, so really, how much do you weigh?"

"A hundred and forty-five pounds."

"How old are you?"

"Oh my God, you're takin' me back to my high school days with this 21 question's game."

"Well I can assure you Yvonne, the school that I attend is a lot tougher than high school, and I'm definitely old enough to buy liquor legally."

Yvonne thought about how she would've hung up on him a long time ago normally, but his voice offered something that she'd been missing for a long time. She smiled at the memory of how she gripped the receiver and continued to trade thoughts with the stranger.

"I'm forty-six."

"Well forty-six is not old Yvonne."

"I suppose it's not, but people will try to flatter you."

"Well, what's wrong with flattery when it's sincere?"

"Good question, but just how can you detect when it's sincere?" She asked.

"Intuition," he answered.

"I'll keep that in mind. So what is it that you do for a living Rob?"

"Well to answer your question briefly, I'm an ex-gang member turned activist, and if you really wanna hear more of my autobiography you'll have to hear it over dinner, so how 'bout it?" Rob woke up from his deep sleep and gave Yvonne a soft kiss on each cheek.

"What's on ya' mind baby?" he asked when he noticed her in deep thought.

"You baby. I'm just sittin' here thinkin' about how you seduced me into your life over the damn phone." They erupted in laughter, then a few moments later, a knock on the door interrupted their conversation.

"Who in the world is this knockin' at my door." Yvonne mumbled as she put her robe on to go answer it.

"It's time for me to get up anyway baby, I gotta be at a NAACP meeting in one hour," said Rob as he stretched, yawned, and climbed his 6-foot dark-skinned slim frame from the bed. Yvonne loved the way he kept his full beard neatly trimmed, and his receding hairline was alright with her, cause it made them look about the same age. Even though she was older than him by seven years.

"Hey yall!" balked Yvonne excitedly when she opened the door and saw Myonly, Love and Ebony. "My three favorite ladies. Yall come on in." Myonly and Love gave Yvonne a big hug.

"Yall smell like strawberries." said Yvonne after they hugged.

"We played baseball with uncle Smoke this morning, then took a bath in my favorite strawberry body wash before we came over here."

Love explained as she stood there dressed in Baby Phat jeans with a matching jacket, with Baby Phat sandals carrying a white Baby Phat purse.

"And who put those long pretty braids in you and your sister's hair?"

"Aunt Ebony," she answered.

"Well aunt Ebony sure did a good job, cause you both look extremely beautiful."

"Thank you," they both replied in unison after Yvonne's compliment.

"Yall want me to make some of my famous turkey sandwiches for yall?"

"Yeah."

"Okay, let me take a shower and I'll get right on it."

Yvonne scurried to the kitchen and put all the ingredients in place. "Damn," she mumbled to herself when she realized she only had white bread, because the girls would only eat wheat bread.

"Ay Eb, can you run to the store and get some wheat bread, cause as of now, that's the only thing that will stop this mission."

"Okay, I'll go right now."

"We wanna' go too," said Myonly and Love as they walked toward the front door.

"Yvonne, we'a be back in a minute okay."

"A'ight," shouted Yvonne from the kitchen.

They jumped in the black Lincoln LS headed for the store.

Fifteen minutes later, they were walking through the grocery store getting way more items than originally planned.

Myonly and Love munched on potato chips after they finished their shopping and made personal jokes about the fat white man who looked just like Santa.

Ebony looked up just as she was approaching her car and caught a glimpse of Smoke riding pass on the passenger side of the BMW she saw earlier. A sudden feeling of disgust came over her, but she quickly told herself to refrain from entertaining that emotion because it would only make matters worse. She hated Smoke's line of work, and she still couldn't believe he was still in the game after the fact they got married, as well as all the drama they'd been through. She was confused and she told herself that being a fool at the expense of love was gettin' old fast.

After she secured Myonly and Love's seatbelt, she slowly backed out of the parking space, errk! She suddenly came to an abrupt stop as another car pulled from another parking space seeming to block her in momentarily.

"What the hell is wrong with people these days?" She angrily mumbled when she realized she barely missed hitting the car. Five seconds later, whack!... everything suddenly went blank for her as the butt of a large caliber weapon slammed into her head near her temple. She made a momentary attempt to pull herself back into lightness, only to realize seconds later it was no use, because her body submitted completely to the blow. And everything remained dark....

One week later.

The two middle-aged black female nurses slightly struggled to restrain Ebony as she awoke from her coma in a frantic state of mind.

"Calm down sweetheart! Please, just calm down. You're alright now, you're in the hospital and no'ones gonna' hurt you."

Ebony's head was wrapped like a mummy, and the pain she felt was excruciating. She slowly calmed down as the realization of the nurses, along with the fact that she was really in the hospital dawned on her. One of the nurses noticed her reaching for her head as if she desperately needed to soothe the pain, so she assisted Ebony in taking two pain relievers.

Yvonne and her fiancé were already there when Ebony woke up, and Yvonne immediately called Smoke to inform him. Fifteen minutes later he stormed through the door with Sheila and Ray Ray right behind him.

"Hey baby," he said before placing a soft kiss on her nose. "How you feelin?"

"Terrible," she mumbled.

"Well don't worry about nothin, the doc said it's just a concussion and ain't no internal damage."

One of the nurses approached her to check her head dressing, and Ebony had a issue.

"First of all, this dressing is not proper, but we will fix that later because I really don't feel like goin' through it now. And second of all, I've seen a million mistakes with yall since I woke up."

The nurses looked at Ebony as if to say, she got some nerve tellin' us how to do our job. Smoke noticed their expressions and intervened.

"Yeah, she knows her shit, she'a nurse too. So listen and learn."

The two nurses turned their noses up and left the room. Ebony glanced up at Sheila and Ray Ray, and from the looks on their faces, she instantly knew something was terribly wrong. Something other than the fact that she had a concussion. Her mind started racing and her sudden rush of adrenaline caused her heart to thump in her chest like an overdosed drug addict.

She had temporarily forgot that the children were with her at the time of the incident. But now, just the memory of it was betraying her in the damnest way because she couldn't remember the conclusion of the day in question. *"What happened to Myonly and Love,"* she thought to herself. *"Are they alright? No, they couldn't be alright, otherwise, Sheila and Ray Ray wouldn't have those dreadful expressions on their faces."* "Oh God, Smoke, please tell me the babies are alright, please! Smoke! Tell me!" She broke down in painful sobs as Smoke tried to console her. Sheila's composure immediately gave way afterwards.

"What happened to my babies!" she shouted. Goddamit

who did this! What did they look like?" Sheila bombarded Ebony with questions, and the confusion in the room grew enormously intense in a matter of minutes. Ray Ray held Sheila back from approaching Ebony while in her frantic state of mind, because he knew she could easily be triggered to attack upon hearing the wrong answers or the wrong tone of voice when it came to issues concerning her babies.

Yvonne quickly joined in and tried to defuse the situation.

"Sheila calm down sweetheart, please, it's gonna be alright. We're gonna get to the bottom of this."

"How in the hell are we gonna get to the bottom of it?" Sheila snapped.

"My babies are missing, and we don't know who in the hell got'em! We don't even-," she struggled to make her final point before completely breaking down. "We don't even know if they're still alive- aaaah!" She bent forward clutching her stomach as her flood of emotions came plunging forward in loud sobs. Smoke continuously tried to calm Ebony down because she was in the same condition as Sheila.

"Ay mama, you and Ray Ray do me a favor," said Smoke as he stood up. "Clear everybody out the room so I can calm her down and possibly get some answers, 'cause we ain't gettin' nowhere like this."

"Yvonne and Ray Ray did just that, and after everyone was out, Ray Ray slipped back in and stood by the door. Smoke looked back at him with a facial expression that said, *"Why are you in here?"* But Ray Ray returned one that said, *"It's self explanatory and I ain't goin nowhere."*

Smoke's eyes quickly formed a truce to solidify their silent understanding, then he slowly turned back to

Ebony.

"I want you to calm down for me baby and listen okay."

Ebony managed to bring her sniffles under better control as Smoke's subtle words sunk in.

"Now check this out Eb, tell me exactly what happened."

Ebony glanced off in the opposite direction from Smoke, with tears still submerged in her hazel brown eyes. She hated the fact that her memory was so vague because she adored Myonly and Love as if they were hers. She cleared her throat, took a deep breath, then spoke in a precise, yet trembling voice as if she didn't wanna miss any details.

"All I remember is making sure Myonly and Love's seatbelts was on, then backing out of the parking space almost hitting another car that pulled directly behind me. I'- I' got a little frustrated, but I had no other choice but to wait until the car moved, so that's what I did. And as I was waiting, I suddenly felt a sharp pain near my temple, and by the time I realized somebody hit me, I went unconscious."

Smoke scooted a little closer to her and gently turned her face toward his by her chin.

"Baby I need you to at least try to remember what the car looked like that blocked you in."

Ebony squirmed and huffed before responding. "Smoke I'm trying to remember; it's just not coming to me."

"Well try a little harder damnit!" Smoke snapped as the answerless situation began to take a toll on him. Ebony's body twitched from his sudden outburst, and Smoke immediately felt bad upon realizing he startled her.

"Listen baby, I'm sorry about snappin at you, but I need answers and I need'em fast. You know we can't bring the police into this 'cause damn near all of us is fugitives. So keep in mind that we gotta handle this on our own. Now do me a big favor and think Eb. Was there anybody familiar, unfamiliar, or just plain suspicious lookin' that you saw in the area that day?"

Ebony closed her eyes and pounded her brain in an effort to remember anything that could possibly provide clues to the situation.

Smoke sat impatiently as two full minutes elapsed in time with Ebony still fishing for thoughts with her eyes closed, and just as he let out a discouraging sigh, she opened her eyes and blurted, "red."

Smoke immediately displayed a confused expression, so she repeated herself with a little more detail. "The car that blocked me in was red."

"Was it a red truck?"

"No, it was a red car, maybe a Stratus or something."

"Okay okay, that's good baby, now we gettin' somewhere. Did you see the driver or any of the passengers?"

"No. I'm positive I didn't see anybody."

"Is you sure baby?"

"Yes I'm sure Smo-," she paused for a moment, then displayed a sarcastic look before continuing.

"But come to think of it, I did see one familiar face in the vicinity."

"Who? Who?" Smoke asked anxiously. Ebony looked directly in his eyes and scornfully replied, "You!"

Smoke was completely caught off guard with her statement. He leaned closer to her with an expression of pure confusion and asked,

"What the fuck is you talkin about Eb?"

"I'm talkin' about you Smoke. I saw you ride pass in the

car with yo' lil friend with the black BMW."

Smoke instantly knew where she was trying to go with the conversation.

"Look Eb, I ain't got time to listen to you whine about my personal business." She quickly cut him off.

"Yo personal business is probably what got us in this predicament in the first fuckin' place!"

The room suddenly fell silent enough to hear a pen drop as Smoke stared at her as if he wanted to slap the truth from her mouth, 'cause in all actuality, he knew her statement was true. And just like the sayin about the truth goes, Smoke learned that the truth really does hurt sometimes. He slowly got up and walked toward the door but was quickly stopped by Ray Ray.

"Whussup dawg, why you grabbin all on me like that?" he asked as he snatched his jacket from Ray Ray's grip.

"Cause nigga you ain't walkin outta here without tellin me who 'da fuck you think is behind this shit!" Ray Ray's eyes were bucked, and the same thick vein that appears on him whenever he gets angry, protruded through the center of his forehead in a snake-like form.

They stared each other down coldly until Smoke realized he definitely owed him an explanation, and that the only way he wouldn't give one would be over Ray Ray's dead body. 'Cause he surely would have to kill him.

"Come on dawg, lets step outside," suggested Smoke before beginning, so they casually stepped over to a neutral corner of the hospital.

"Check this out dawg, you know I still been gettin my grind on with 'da work, and the scene out here on that tip is a little different 'cause most of the gang members control how the work gets distributed. Now, to make a long story short, I recently bumped heads with a blood leader name Damu because he tried to dictate who I sell my shit too. He mainly don't want me sellin nothin to no crips, and when I let him know he barkin' up the wrong tree, he didn't take that to kindly. So I think he might be behind this shit, and if he is, I'ma make an example out of his bitch ass, I promise."

Ray Ray stared at Smoke with a blank expression for a seemingly long 60 seconds before responding to anything he said.

"Dawg, first of all, I can't believe yo' dumb ass is still fuckin wit' dat' shit. And on top of that, you got my babies snatched up on some dumb shit pertaining to some bitch ass drugs, AND YOU KNOW! HOW I FEEL ABOUT DRUGS AND THE MUTHAFUCKAS WHO DEAL'EM!" he shouted. "Now you know I'm about to turn this muthafucka upside down lookin' for my babies. All I want you to do is show me who dude is, and stay the fuck out my way, let's bounce..."

CHAPTER 3

Ray Ray gripped the AR-15 that laid across his lap tightly as Smoke cruised through the blood neighborhood at low speed. Several gang members wearing red bandanas delivered mean stares as the unfamiliar car cruised by. Smoke suddenly hit the brakes when he noticed Damu's little sister. She was dark complected like Damu and wore corn rows to the back.

Her eighteen-year-old tomboyish frame, along with her same sex preference made her look more like a boy than a girl. She stood there with her pants saggin, holdin' hands with a light-skinned female who wore a short burgundy jean skirt, with a pasty dark red lipstick.

"Ay Damiesha," Smoke called out to her, but she ignored him. She stood there as if she didn't hear him, so he called out again with a little more authority this time.

"Damiesha let me holla atchu for a minute." This time, she turned toward her girlfriend and planted a sloppy tounge kiss on her, then adjusted the weapon in her pants and approached the car.

"Whatchu want over here fool. I heard you was workin' wit' da' enemy," she blurted.

"Damn!" said Smoke. "Good news sho'l travel fast. And why in the fuck is a nigga lil sister all in a nigga bidness anyway?"

"Cause I'm knee deep in this shit just as deep as he is,

and I can hold mine just as good as any nigga out here, nigga!" she squawked as she gripped her gun through her flannel shirt and gave Smoke a sarcastic nod.

"A'ight Damiesha, I know you 'bout yours, but I ain't come over here to challenge yo' street credibility. I'm lookin' for yo' brother, have you seen him?"

"Naw, and I wouldn't tell you if I did, nigga!"

"Check this out you lil dickless bitch!" Ray Ray snapped.

"Ain't nobody come over here to be playin' wit' yo' lil hoe-ass, now have you seen the nigga or not?"

"Fuck you ol' busta-ass nigga, who 'da fuck you think you is?"

Before she could get the rest of the sentence out of her mouth, Ray Ray was out the car with his hand gripped around her throat.

He took the Ruger from her pants and pressed it against her pussy.

"Now you want me to give you a reminder that you got a pussy between yo' legs bitch. Huh, you lil once-a-month-bleedin' bitch. Just keep runnin' 'dat mouth and I'ma give you what you lookin' fo.' Now I'ma ask you one mo' time, have you seen yo' bitch ass brother?"

"Nawww," she squealed through Ray Ray's tight grip.

"Now that's more like it lil bitch. And tell them three clowns that keep creepin' up toward us, I'ma empty this clip in yo' ass if they don't get 'da fuck back." She waved for the men to get back. And when they did, Ray Ray let her go, then slapped her across the face with the Ruger. He was about to turn and get in the car, but instinctively he glanced around the area and quickly thought to himself, *"Hell naw, these niggas will light our shit up before we can get off the block."*

"Get up bitch." He opened the door and shoved her in

the back seat then climbed in beside her. He placed the gun under her chin, then ordered Smoke to drive.

When they made it a couple blocks away, Smoke pulled over and Ray Ray dragged her out. He pulled her close to him and snarled, "Tell yo' brother he fuckin' wit the wrong one." Then shoved her to the pavement and got back in the car. Damiesha gave a cold stare as Smoke pulled off.

"Dawg, why 'da fuck did you do that?" asked Smoke in an angry tone.

"Man if Damu really is the one who got Myonly and Love, ain't no tellin what 'da nigga might do now."

"Man fuck 'dat nigga!" Ray Ray shouted.

"I shoulda' killed that bitch. Now don't get me wrong nigga, I hope and pray the nigga ain't did nothin' stupid to my babies, but I look at it like this, he gon' do what he gon' do anyway. Now keep drivin' til we find this nigga."

Myonly held her sister tight as they sat in the spacious room sobbing and frightened about their ordeal. The same man approached them at 2 o'clock pm, just as he'd been doing every day since their abduction. He was short, medium built, and wore a black ski mask with matching gloves whenever he was in their presence. He sat the bag of McDonald's on the table beside the other two- and three-day old untouched McDonald's bags.

The man casually lit a cigarette, then pointed at the food and said, "eat!' then slowly walked back out the room, locking the door behind him. Myonly and Love ignored the man and continued to cry and hold each other tight....

Later on that night, Ray Ray and Smoke stopped by Yvonne's house to check on Sheila. When they walked in, the first thing Ray Ray noticed was Sheila on her knees crouched over in the corner. He ran over to her in a hurry to see what was wrong.

"Whussup baby, what's wrong?"

"Nothin' baby," said Sheila as she looked up at him with swollen eyes from her constant crying.

"I'm just prayin. I embraced the Sunni Muslim faith while I was in prison, and this is how we pray."

Ray Ray displayed a puzzled look on his face before responding.

"Oh, okay. Well do what you gotta' do baby." He turned toward Smoke and they left right back out the door. They pulled up at Kay loke's house ten minutes later.

The neighborhood seemed rather quiet, and the usual crowd of people that occupied those streets were nowhere around. Kay walked out the house with a gloomy expression as the streetlight glared off his shiny bald head.

"Whut up cuz?" he greeted Smoke.

"Ain't nothing dawg, whuddup? And why it look like a damn ghost-town around here?"

"Cuz you ain't heard?"

"Heard what?"

"Man three of my lil soldiers got slumped tonight. The police just left about 15 minutes ago. That bitch-ass nigga Damu came through here talkin' 'bout it's officially on. He told me to make sure I give you this message,

"When it rains it pours."

"Yeah we'a see about that," replied Smoke.

Kay demonstrated with hand gestures as he further

explained.

"Cuz I had the infra red beam on that nigga, then I happened to look down at my chest off instinct, and his boy already had one dancin' on my shit so I had to freeze game. That's when he gave his lil speech and left. Damn I let them niggas kill my soldiers cuz." ... K-loke spoke with grief as he thought about it.

"But that's a'ight, 'cause It's on whenva' I see that nigga again."

Kay loke's younger brother Fatts walked out on the porch clutching his head. He had short curly hair, a caramel brown complexion, and weighed almost five hundred pounds. His 5'9 frame looked as if it suffered from carrying so much weight. And he always sounded like he was in a deep sleep snoring while he was wide awake.

"Whuddup Fatts?" Smoke spoke.

"Ain't nothin man. Just them sucka's comin' through here on that sucka shit. A bullet grazed my head while I was in the crib tryin to get my groove on with Juanita, but I'm a'ight."

Smoke's eyes lit up playfully before responding.

"You mean basehead Juanita who can suck a golf-ball through a garden hose?" Fatts laughed before replying,

"Yeah her."

"Well at least you had a pro witcha dawg. And the gap between her teeth seem to make things so much better."

"How you know Smoke?" asked Fatts as he displayed a wide grin.

"Oh, I heard it through the grapevine." They all burst out laughin' accept Ray Ray.

"Ay dawg, let's bounce. We got a bitch-ass nigga to find." Ray Ray snarled. Kay loke walked up to Smoke and asked.

"Whussup with yo' boy?" Smoke glanced off, looking at nothing or no-one in particular before responding.

"That's really what I came over here to holla at you about dawg. His two little girls got snatched up the same day Damu tripped out about me sellin' work to yo' set. And we think he had somethin' to do with it."

Immediate silence followed Smoke's statement, then a fearful expression instantly appeared on Kay's face. He stood there looking puzzled as if he was suddenly lost for words.

"Whuddup dawg, what's on ya' mind?" asked Smoke in a concerned tone when he realized something wasn't right. Kay let out a heavy sigh before responding, as if he had to release a pressure bubble for what he was about to say next.

"Check this out cuz, a few years ago, Damu's set went to war with another mud set on the northside over Damu tryin' to be a gorilla and tryna' run shit like always. Anyway, the beef went on for about three months strong, and just when it looked like Damu was gon' lose the battle, he flipped the script and upped the stakes of the war." Another heavy sigh sounded off before Kay continued.

"Cuz, a little boy and a little girl about the ages of nine and seven came up missing from the other set, and three weeks later all they found was-," Kay paused for a moment before he continued.

"What dawg? All they found was what?" asked Smoke desperately.

Kay looked him straight in the eyes with visible signs of regret and continued,

"Cuz, all they found was the two kid's headless bodies with a note attached." Smoke's facial expression was now identical to Kay's. He rubbed his head then looked away in frustration, but quickly turned right back toward Kay with a bodily expression that said, *"tell me the rest while I'm braced for it,"* then asked,

"What did the note say dawg?"

Kay stood there staring as if he didn't hear him.

"Dawg!" Smoke shouted from frustration.

"What da' fuck did it say!" Kay stared blankly for a moment, not really wanting to discuss it any further as he thought about the same possible fate of Damu's two new victims. But he quickly realized that this wasn't the time to be sentimental or reminiscent, it was time for straight forward answers to straight forward questions, so he reluctantly answered.

"When it rains it pours. And cuz, the police never did find the kids heads."

"Fuck!" yelled Smoke.

"Let's ride Ray Ray, I'll get atchu later Loke, hit me if you hear anything." Kay stood there calmly as several more of his gang-members pulled up ready for whatever. He shook his head negatively and threw up the deuces as he watched Smoke speed up the street in the black Lincoln LS in a distraught manner.

As they navigated throughout L.A. in search of Damu or any clues to his whereabouts, Ray Ray's mind drifted off to places that will forever be engraved in his memory, *"Where 'da money at big Ray?" asked the gunman. Nigga if I gotta ask you one mo' time, I'ma blow yo' shit out. Nigga this ain't all of it, where's the rest? Oh, you wanna act stupid, okay, Boom! Big Ray screamed as his common law wife's brains flung out her head and her limp body dropped to the floor. After securing half a million from big Ray, another shot was fired, this time killing Ray Ray's best friend lil Ron."* Ray

Ray squirmed uncomfortably in his seat as the violent images constantly flashed through his mind. Small beads of sweat appeared on his nose as he thought about how he lost his mother, father, and best friend in the same incident.

"Those drugs dealin' muthafucka's," he mumbled to himself as the car glided through the streets. Bo-Bo and Spade had robbed and killed his parents just to settle a drug debt with another drug dealer, and it ate Ray Ray up inside whenever he thought about it, like now. *"Ray Ray, do you recognize any of these men?" asked the detective conducting the police line-up.* Ray Ray remembered how he stood there at the age of eleven with the power in his tongue to put Bo-Bo and Spade away forever, but he didn't because he had something else in mind. *"Ray Ray, help me put these bastards away," pleaded the black detective. "I don't condone the fact that your father was a heavy heroin dealer, but I always had to respect his character because he was a straight-up guy. He was the kind of guy that would tell you to your face, "I'll never snitch, so don't ever ask me too."* "I hate drug dealers!" is what Ray Ray screamed at the age of eleven as he took in what would be the last time he saw Bo-Bo and Spade until adulthood. His thoughts flipped from anger to satisfaction as he thought about the fact that time allowed him to catch up and murder Bo-Bo and Spade. He felt they were truly responsible for his past occupation. All the drug dealers that he robbed and murdered seemed to all reflect back to Bo-Bo and Spade. Maybe it was because of the convenience of being able to point the finger. Or maybe it wasn't. He questioned himself. But despite what it was that drove him to it, Bo-Bo and Spade definitely played a key role. And despite what other miscellaneous elements that played key roles in his lifestyle, the hood seemed to always get the last laugh. *"Spell wonderful." "Wonderful," pronounced Love outloud before she spoke into the mic. "W-O-N-D-E-R-F-U-L, wonderful." "Correct," said the spelling bee instructor before she called out another word for Love to spell.*

"Colonel, spell Colonel."

Love pronounced the word again before proceeding. "Colonel." Then suddenly she paused and stared out at the audience in silence as if something was wrong...a few moments after her strange behavior, the instructor cleared her throat as if to say, "snap out of it," then asked, "Did you not understand the word sweetheart?" "Yes mam," answered Love.

"Okay then, let's proceed, spell Colonel."

Love pronounced the word outloud again, but still became hesitant afterwards. "Are you alright honey?" asked the black female instructor with the Brazilian accent. Love remained silent for another full minute, then looked at Ray Ray in the audience and shouted. "Daddy, what does Colonel start with, a K or a C?" A small wave of laughter from the audience followed her statement.

Ray Ray stood up before responding, "babygirl, the lady asked you the question, not me. So give it a little more thought, and whatever you think it is, just spell it okay baby."

"But daddy."

"No but's Love. How can you go wrong with our motto?"

Love shrugged her shoulders and whispered, "I don't know."

"Well I do," answered Ray Ray. "Now what's our motto?" Love smiled then answered. "Chances make champions."

"That's right baby, now spell the word."

She sighed deeply, then began. "K-O-L-O-N-A-L"

"Incorrect," said the instructor...Aw's of sympathy could

immediately be heard from most of the people in the audience as Love lowered her head toward the floor. Ray Ray quickly spoke up. "Love!" he called out firmly. "What did daddy tell you about dealin' with disappointments?" Love answered in a barely audible tone. "Always with your head up."

"That's right, now put yours where it needs to be." She slowly lifted her head. "Now after all that's happened here today, what did we learn?"

Love looked at her daddy with an expression of confidence, then answered. "Chances still make champions." The crowd immediately gave her a standing ovation as Love stood there smiling at Ray Ray who smiled in return. Ray Ray's thoughts were still ping-ponging in his mind as he and Smoke navigated through traffic... *As the ambulance workers placed the deceased hit and run victim on the stretcher, the nine-year-old victim's mother was shocked to see her only son go. The Brazilian boy lived on the same block as Ray Ray. And being that Myonly had played with him on several occasions, she was also sad to see him go. Her emotions showed a few days after the incident while sitting on Ray Ray's lap eating ice cream at the zoo.*

She became quizzical with him like she always did when something bothered her. "Daddy, why do people die?"

Her question was unexpected, and Ray Ray didn't quite know how to answer it. But he was persistent when it came to answering his daughter's questions, no matter how odd or complicated they'd be. He would always find a logical answer. He paused momentarily as the giant question from his little girl bounced around in his head, then calmly stated, "To give others a chance to live baby, that's why people die."

"Damn!" yelled Ray Ray outloud as he concluded his barrage of thoughts, then he suddenly blurted,

"Ay dawg, shoot to the liquor stoe' so I can get some

Seagram's extra dry in my life, fast."

Smoke glanced over at him with a thoughtful expression and mumbled,

"I feel you dawg," then pulled over at the nearest liquor store. He put the car in park and attempted to get out but stopped and turned back toward Ray Ray instead.

"Dawg, let me ask you something personal, and please don't take offense homie, this me. Anyway, how in the fuck did you get a guard uniform, and a blueprint of the joint to be able to walk up in that bitch and walk back out with yo' wife?"

Ray Ray nonchalantly turned toward him wearing an expression that indicated he'd asked a stupid question, then replied.

"Money talk, bullshit walk. That's the world we live in dawg, act like you know."

Smoke smirked with a wide grin, then went in the liquor store to get what they came for.

Thirty minutes later, as they were still lurking through the dark streets in predator mode, Ray Ray unexpectedly yelled out,

"Stop the car dawg!" he turned toward Smoke frantically because he felt that he wasn't stopping fast enough.

"Hit the brakes on this muhfucka dawg, hurry up!"

Skrrrrrrr!!! Ray Ray leaped out the car as it slid to a screeching stop. He pulled the 45 automatic from his waist as he ran full speed toward the black man wearing a black skull-cap with an all black kaki suit. The man moved methodically and had no idea he was being pursued as he walked toward the entrance of a convenient store... Ray Ray's adrenaline was elevated as he moved in closer. He gripped the gun tighter, then in one smooth motion, he grabbed the man's arm and aggressively spinned him around. Which caused him to release his grip from the two little girls who he previously walked hand in hand with.

"Myonly! Love!" Ray Ray shouted frantically as he stood there breathing heavy with the gun pressed against the man's forehead.

"What th-."

"Shut the fuck up nigga!" Ray Ray lashed out as the man attempted to say something.

"Uhhh, daddy! daddy!" the two small girls simultaneously began to cry.

"I'm here babies, daddy's here!" Ray Ray assured as he reached for them.

The girls quickly ran away from him, and each one held a tight grip on the subdued man's legs.

"Man just take the money or whateva' you want, but please don't hurt my babies." The man pleaded with Ray Ray.

The girls continued to cry and inch further behind the man. They just wanted to get away from the gunman who held the large caliber weapon to their father's head.

A sudden expression of confusion appeared on Ray Ray's face. He focused closer on the little girls, and it was then that he knew the liquor, along with his desperate mental state was the blame for his crazed actions.

Smoke immediately noticed when Ray Ray realized he was at fault, so he remained calm in hopes that everything would smooth-out from that point on. Ray Ray lowered the weapon and slowly began to back away.

"Silly muthafucka," mumbled the man as he watched the intensity start to settle in Ray Ray's demeanor.

Ray Ray suddenly stopped, and the mask of anger

reappeared as the man's insult registered in his mind.

"Whut da' fuck you just say nigga?"

The man remained silent, and this infuriated Ray Ray even more.

"I'ma ask you one mo' time dawg. Whut da' fuck did you just say?"

"Nothin' man, I was just sayin' how this is a silly situation that needs to come to a peaceful end."

Ray Ray leaped forward and slapped blood from his mouth with the gun, then just as quickly aimed it at his face and discharged the weapon. But the swift shift of Ray Ray's arm by Smoke allowed the bullet to miss dude by inches.

"Dawg chill!" yelled Smoke as he held Ray Ray's arm tight. "Let me handle this nigga!" Smoke grimaced as he released Ray Ray and charged toward the man.

He threw a serious combination of punches to his face, sending him tumbling to the ground hard. Smoke crouched over and grabbed him by the shirt, then delivered a steady string of stiff punches with his right fist 'til he heard the man's jaw break. His daughters were terrified and crying hysterically as Smoke continued to mangle their father.

Smoke kicked and stomped him in the face as he cursed and yelled all kinds of obscenities.

"You stupid muthafucka! You was home free but yo' dumb ass had to open yo' mouth. And got the nerves to call my homie a silly muthafucka, and you the silliest muthafucka out here."

Smoke delivered one more hard kick to the man's head, knocking him unconscious. Then glanced at his crying daughters before turning towards Ray Ray.

"Let's bounce dawg, fuck dat nigga."

Smoke felt bad about the fact that he had to batter the man in front of his daughters. But he mentally noted, it wasn't the first time, and definitely wouldn't be the last.

CHAPTER 4

"Okay, listen up people," yelled special agent Burns as he pointed at the pinned-up photos on the white portable board.

"This individual was recently busted out of a female state penitentiary in Cold Water Michigan. Her name is Sheila Thompson, and she's the wife of this individual here," he pointed at Ray Ray's photo then continued.

"For those of you who are not familiar with him, I'll briefly inform you. He's a fugitive that we've been chasing for the last few years heavily. And he's wanted in connection with the slaying of federal agent Nathaniel Lawson. He's the leader of a notorious gang who we use to refer to as 'The Get Flat Crew', but upon further investigation we found out they're known in the streets as 'G-Riders'. Mr. Thompson is also wanted for questioning on numerous murders that their gang is suspected of being directly involved in. Now we believe he's resurfaced, and that he's responsible for his wife's successful escape. So as of this minute I want you all to turn the city of Detroit upside down searching for any clues, from the largest to the smallest, that could possibly lead us to them. Stop at my desk on the way out for copies of their mugshots and profile sheets, you're dismissed."

CHAPTER 5

The juvenile gang-members sat attentively in the auditorium of the all-male juvenile detention center as Rob continued his lecture.

"It must be really lonely being angry at yourselves brothers. Angry because of the fact that you let something so simple become so complicated. At one point in time your lives were simple. Simple as in waking up in the morning, eating, interacting, and sleeping. But somewhere along that road, your complacency allowed you to open the door to a negative reality. And in turn, it came at the price of compromising your peace.

Now let's reflect back for a moment, because I can imagine how the transition felt for you in the beginning. I'll bet it was exciting, intoxicating, and adventurous all in the same breath. You probably felt powerful and unrestricted, 'cause we all know that there ain't no feelin' like the feeling of being wanted or needed by somebody. You felt that you finally belonged, and it was a natural high in itself. But let's look at the repercussions of your re-birth. Something was taken away, as if it was surgically removed. But brothers, I'm here to let yall know that it doesn't have to be surgically replaced. It can be replaced through knowledge, understanding and knowing who you truly are and what your true purpose in life is.

I look at everyone in this room today and all I see is

victims of a man-made circumstance. I know it's not all your fault brothers, because I was just like yall. I was on the frontline too. I went through the initiation, the puttin' in work, the shakedowns and harassment by the law, and everything that comes with growing up in a black underprivileged predicament. So don't think I came here today to tell yall it's all yall fault to end up in places like this, cause I know better. The science of it goes way back and it's much bigger than us wavin' a few colors around and beefin' over turf.

For example, let's briefly go back to 1862. There was a so-called amendment that was issued by President Abraham Lincoln, entitled, 'Emancipation Proclamation'. Most of you probably heard your parents talk about how this piece of legislation freed the slaves, when in all actuality that's the furthest thing from the truth. First of all, Lincoln waited until things became politically correct inside the war before he even issued the order. Why, because he had a hidden agenda, like most politicians do. And the most memorable words to the people were, *'all slaves held in areas in rebellion against the union are free'.*

But ask yourselves, what did this really amount too? Nothing, because Lincoln had freed the slaves in the confederacy where his authority wasn't recognized. Not to mention, by speaking of areas in rebellion, he didn't include the five slave-holding border states. Nor did this order apply to captured southern lands already under union control. Now let's ask ourselves another logical question. What was the purpose of this proclamation that freed practically nobody? It was simply propaganda, just another money scheme in disguise. It was all based around the north deciding to tax the south for their cotton, rice, and a bunch of other consumer goods.

Which is what started the civil war in the first place. And we all know that in wars, you need expendable soldiers. And what better soldier to put on the front line than slaves who've been told their free.

What Lincoln gave us was the illusion of freedom, and it was documented in history under a false pretense. Just like ya' boy Christopher Columbus, whom the historians say discovered America, when it was really a man named Amerigo Despucci. By the time Christopher showed up, his only intentions was to do what his entourage did best, steal the land from whoever was here first." Rob suddenly held his hand up before he continued.

"But I'm not gonna' get too deeply into that today brothers, 'cause it makes my blood pressure go berserk."

A few of the attendees clapped and laughed at his truthful statement, then settled down a few moments later so he could continue.

"Brothers, basically what I'm tellin yall is something that you've already heard from some of our past scholars, so I know that this information is not new to a lot of you. But those of you who haven't heard it, take it upon yourselves to dig deeper and do further research. Then compare it to what you've heard today and use your own judgment from there. The powers that be are using the same system against us. The clicks, the crews, the gangs, or whatever, we've all been given the illusion of freedom. Yeah we free alright, free to kill each other off and make it easier for them to bring a new social order to the world....

Viable maturity is not an overnight process, so I don't expect a sudden change in yall. But I truly do hope and pray that you make a great effort toward that change. 'Cause life is what you make it, it all starts with you."

The teenage offenders all applauded him

simultaneously as he concluded his lecture. The detention officers immediately walked down the center of the aisle in preparation to escort the juvenile's back to their living quarters. Rob displayed an irritable expression as he watched the Bloods sit on one side of the room, and the Crips on the other. They all suddenly stood up at the officer's command, with orders to keep their hands at their sides during the transit route. No exceptions. Rob quickly approached the lieutenant who was in charge of the operation.

"Excuse me sir, may I have a word with you?"

"Yeah, what's up?"

Rob cleared his throat before continuing.

"Listen, I need you to do me a big favor. I'm here because I'm trying to promote gang unity, not gang separation. You understand. I want these kids to realize they are not animals, and that they can be in here in the midst of each other and interact in a civilized manner, without negative interference. So, what I'm asking of you, is to let me conduct a five-minute peace demonstration by letting each side shake hands in an orderly fashion, then you can escort them back to their quarters and my work here is done."

The heavyset darkskinned officer breathed a sigh of annoyance before responding.

"I don't think that's a good idea sir."

"Aw come on Lt. it's only gonna be a simple handshake, I'll take full responsibility."

"That's easy for you to say when it's not truly your neck on the line, it's mine. And it seems to me that you don't understand the fact that this is a maximum-security facility, and these kids are not as innocent and sweet as you'd like to believe. They are cold hearted criminals, and they live for the chance to get what they call 'stripes' every chance that they get."

Rob stepped closer to the Lt. when he realized his request had officially turned into a debate.

"Lt. I'm aware of everything you just mentioned, 'cause like I said in my lecture, I use to be one of them. So the first thing that I want you to understand about me is the fact that I'm sincere about what I do. And I feel that us, the so-call sensible adults, constantly breed the bullshit that arouses their behavior because we constantly remind them of the monsters they've become, while indirectly glorifying it at the same time. It's like we feed the negative energy whenever we beef up the security and go through the extra measures to contain or restrain them, 'cause all it basically does is compliment the danger in them.

Which in turn, only makes them feel that doin' dirt is the cool thing to do. It's time for us to turn that around Lt. Let's show them that we'd be more impressed by a handshake instead of a drive-by. It's gotta' start somewhere."

The Lt. glanced out at the several hundred young gang members as they stood there with officers in position to be escorted back to their units.

His eyes slowly scanned the crowd as he pondered on everything he'd just discussed with Rob. He felt that Rob had a point and thought about how he would always give some of the youngsta's positive advice whenever he felt the need to. He was considered a good officer in the facility and would give some of the inmates a much-needed break from time to time if the incident wasn't too serious. But, overall, he was still known for being a no-nonsense type of person... He stood there a few seconds

longer, contemplating, before suddenly blurting out,
"Escort'em back to their quarters! Now!!"

Rob was highly disappointed, but not as disappointed as the young Blood member Damon who was anxiously anticipating the interaction so he could attack the young Crip from Kay's set. He'd been watching him the whole night, and all the while, he reflected back on how his older brother Damu had sent the word from the streets that it was officially law to ride on anybody from K-Loc's set whenever the opportunity presented itself. Damon had more than forty homies there in the auditorium with the same agenda. And if the Lt. would've okayed the demonstration, he would've certainly been out of a job that night. It would've been an all-out war in there. One that would have required a lot of overtime and manpower to bring under control.

CHAPTER 6

As the car came to a stop, Ray Ray woke up out of a brief sleep.

"What is you doin' dawg? Why we back at yo' house? Let's ride nigga, we ain't through lookin' for my babies."

Smoke displayed a sincere expression before responding.

"Dawg, don't you think we had enough drama for one night. We gotta' get some rest so we can go at this shit strong tomorrow, so chill man. And besides, your wife is in there in need of comfort right now."

"Dawg don't run no shit to me about what my wife is in need of." Ray Ray snarled.

"Don't you think I know that. You just worry about what yours need and keep mine out'cha mouth. And what I can't understand is why in the fuck don't nobody know where that nigga Damu live."

Smoke answered undoubtfully.

"Cause he never stay in one place too long, he stick and move the way we use too. And you know as well as I do, with that kind of discipline, a guy can get real far in the game."

"Yeah, but only so far," advised Ray Ray.......

After stepping from the shower and drying off, Ray Ray strolled in the bedroom and gently sat on the bed beside

Sheila. He slid his Sean John robe off and began to put lotion on...

Sheila unexpectedly sat up and assisted him. She casually took the bottle from his hand, then squirted a small amount in her palm. Ray Ray slightly motioned forward from the sudden chill as she applied it to his back. She could tell that he'd been drinking, and that the stress had taken a toll on him. His three-day old scruffy beard told part of the story.

"I thought you was sleep baby."

"Yeah, I was, but I had to get up because it'll be time for me to pray in five minutes." Ray Ray turned toward her before curiously asking,

"Baby what made you turn to that particular religion?"

Sheila re-adjusted her sitting before answering.

"Well, first of all, I had a lot of quiet reflection time in prison. And after I was introduced to Islam, I used those times of solitude to evaluate who I was as a person, then discern what predicament my soul was in. I eventually came to the conclusion that it was time for my soul-searching to come to an end, because I'd finally found something that touched the core of my heart and made me feel complete. Baby it's a beautiful doctrine, and the literature is truly amazing. We pray five times a day to Allah as a sign of homage for his mercifulness, as well as repentance for all of our imperfections."

"Well let me ask you this baby, what do it mean when yall be sayin asa-, asail'" Sheila held her hand up as she bent forward laughin' at his goofin up the word.

"Baby the correct way to say it is assalam aleikum. It's Arabic, and it means may peace be unto you. Walaikum assalam means peace be unto you also. And even if you're not muslim, it's still alright for you to return the greeting with walaikum assalam, because it basically demonstrates courtesy."

Ray Ray was impressed by Sheila's explanation of the new chapter in her life, and he mentally noted that she never ceased to amaze him. She was such a strong-willed woman, and he was used to her approaching every endeavor with the highest level of sincerity. He dosed off as he watched her perform the prayer on a prayer-rug in the corner of the room.......

The following day, as Sheila prepared breakfast for everybody, Ebony entered the kitchen and went in the refrigerator for some cranberry juice. She glanced at Sheila in a timid manner because they hadn't spoke since the confrontation at the hospital. Ebony was aware that Sheila was bitter with her because of the situation with Myonly and Love. And Ebony felt completely uncomfortable being in the same room with her. Sheila felt that it was Ebony's carelessness that got her babies kidnapped, and she also felt uncomfortable being in the same room with Ebony. The tension in the room was so thick, that one could cut it with a knife.

Ebony's hand slightly trembled as she tried to hurry up with her task so she could get out of Sheila's space.

Tsshhh!!

The glass of juice suddenly slipped from her hand and shattered on the floor creating a small mess.

"Damn!" she uttered as she scurried off to get a broom for the glass, and a mop for the spill....

When she returned, Sheila had already grabbed the small broom that sat in the corner beside one of the counters, and slowly swept the glass in a small pile throughout the splattered juice. Ebony quickly provided a dustpan, then rung the pinesol mixed water from the mop and cleaned up the small spill....

A few moments afterwards, she exhaled a deep breath, then approached Sheila passively.

Thanks Sheila. I- I really appreciate your help girl., I'm just plain clumsy today." She laughed a little in hopes that Sheila would join in. But she didn't, so Ebony glanced around the room in a fidgety manner as her mind quickly searched for another approach.

After giving it a few seconds of thought, she decided to just say what was on her heart to say whether Sheila accepted it or not.

"Uh, Sheila listen. I know you feel that I was responsible for what happened to the babies. And in a sense, maybe I was." She paused momentarily.

"Maybe I shoulda' rammed the car that blocked me in. Or maybe I shoulda' had a gun just in case some gangsta's would wanna come and do harm to a simple person like me." Ebony's voice began to crackle as she went on.

"Or maybe I shoulda' had the babies duck down as soon as they got in the car so nobody could see them 'til we got home. Sheila, I don't watch my rearview mirror for blocks and blocks to see if I'm being followed. Know what I mean?... What I'm tryin to say is, I'm not a gangsta, and neither are you Sheila. So how are we supposed to know about taking gangsta-precautions when we are just ordinary women? Well let me rephrase that, we were ordinary women, but now we're something else, thanks to our husbands. Our husbands are gangsta's Sheila, not us. Our husbands lead that lifestyle, and we are the ones who suffer the repercussions of it. And I'm sick of it!"

Ebony yelled as the tears began to roll down her face.

"I loved your babies more than you know, and it kills me to even think about what happened to them. Sheila, I-

I'm sorry!"

Ebony broke down crying, and the compassion that Sheila felt at that moment caused her to open her arms and embrace Ebony. They both held each other tight and cried together as Yvonne and Rob stood in one of the entrance ways to the kitchen feeling joyful about the truce...........

Later on that day, as Ray Ray and Smoke rode silently in the car, Smoke dialed K-loke's cell number. He answered after four rings.

"Whut up cuz?"

"Ain't nothing up dawg, I'm just callin to see if you heard anything on ol'boy's whereabouts."

"Naw cuz I ain't heard shit, but trust me, my soldiers is on it. But check this out cuz, even though we got this lil situation goin' on, I still got bills to pay. So I desperately need you to hit me wit' ten mo' thangs like now."

"Dawg ain't no haps right now, shit is on hold 'til we clear this shit up."

"Aw come on cuz, this me, and I'm hurtin right now. I need you 911 baby. Just hit me one moe' time 'til we get our problem straightened out, and I can maintain from there 'til better days."

Smoke paused for a moment as he thought about how much money Kay's been spending with him over the years. He also thought about the stiff consequences he would have to face if Ray Ray found out he was doin' a drug deal with him in the car. He didn't like sittin' on drugs to long, and he really didn't like passin up money. So after giving it a little more thought, he agreed. He pushed a cd in the cd player and turned up the volume on Beanie Sigal's classic *'Whatcha life like.'* in an effort to muffle the rest of his conversation from Ray Ray.

"A'ight dawg, meet me at the nearest Quick-n-split restaurant in twenty minutes."

"Bet cuz, holla."

Smoke drove to one of his safe houses and told Ray Ray to come in with him so he could show him something. When they went in, Smoke went to the back room and returned with a black duffle-bag. He opened it and produced two brand-new Mac-tens.

"Dawg, check these out, these muhfucka's straight. I been thinkin' about getting a couple for myself but I ain't trippin' 'cause I already got a arsenal of shit. I gotta' run these to Kay right quick 'cause they his. So check this out, we gon' leave our heat here until we drop these off. 'Cause it be a lot of hook ridin' in the area where I'm 'spose to meet him at, a'ight?"

Ray Ray didn't like the idea of leaving his weapons, but he understood so he agreed. They put the guns up, and as they were headed back out the door, Smoke suddenly stopped.

"Damn, I forgot to put the extra clips in the bag, I'll be right back." He ran to the back with the duffle bag and quickly replaced the mac-10's with the ten kilos of cocaine. He got in the car and turned the volume up on Beanie Siegal then pulled off.........

15 minutes later.

Smoke pulled up in the parking lot of the restaurant beside the blue camero Kay was drivin. His brother Fatts sat on the passenger side looking as if his body was big enough to occupy both front seats. Smoke approached Kay with the duffle-bag, and Kay slapped five with him and climbed back in the camero. It was a rule for them to never socialize for more than five minutes after a drug deal, and Smoke would always pick up the money for the drugs thirty minutes afterwards.

As they both pulled out in traffic, Smoke's heart skipped a beat when he glanced to the left of him and saw Damu's red hummer, along with Damu and a few of his boys talking to some skankish lookin' chicks.

"Whut da fu- "He speed-dialed Kay's cellphone.

"Hello."

"Dawg look to yo' left! Hurry up!"

As Kay looked over, Smoke was already making a u-turn in the middle of the busy street. And soon as his turn was complete, the lights from the L.A.P.D were flashing in his rearview.

"Damn!" Smoke grimaced as he pulled over to the curb....

As Kay completed his u-turn, he drove right pass Smoke as if he didn't know him.

"Baker Adam six this is Baker Adam four, pull that blue camero over that's headed your way."

"Ten four," responded the other unit as it pulled behind Kay with the lights on.

"Damn, why he pull over wit' all that work in the car." Smoke thought to himself.

The white officer approached the driver-side of the black Lincoln LS, while the Spanish officer approached the passenger-side.

"Let me see your license, registration, and proof of insurance."

Smoke casually handed the officer the credentials that he already had in his hand by the time he made it to the car.

"Have you been drinking buddy?" asked the officer.

"No sir, I don't drink."

"What about PCP, you been smokin' that shit?"

"No sir, I don't indulge in that either."

"Well why in the hell did you make that dangerous fuckin' u-turn, don't you know you could've killed somebody. And that goes for your asshole buddy up there in that blue camero too."

"Excuse me sir, but that's not my buddy, I don't know dude."

"Aw cut the bullshit, do you think I'm a fuckin rookie? Now the best thing for you to do is shut the fuck up and pray that your credentials come up clean." The officer walked back to the squad car to check out the info, then returned ten minutes later. He handed Smoke everything back, then asked both of them to step out the vehicle.

"Why is that officer, what's the problem?"

"The problem is, you ask too many silly questions. Now step out the fuckin' car so I can find out if you have any open liquor in there." Smoke knew it was a bunch of bullshit but being that he was clean and his alius was good, he co-operated.

"Now step back here to my squad car and stand there 'til I say otherwise."

The white officer spent ten minutes searching the car, then returned empty handed. Smoke glanced up the street at Damu as he flirted with the most attractive girl within the bunch. Damu never noticed them, and Ray Ray was overly anxious to get to him.

"Place both of your hands on the hood and spread your legs." The officer demanded. Smoke and Ray Ray complied.

"This looks like an expensive jacket man. Who's it made by?" the officer asked as he patted Smoke down.

"It's made by Al Wissam."

"Hmf," the officer smirked as he continued to search him.

"And look at your partner over there, he's wearing a jacket and pants that says State Property. And if my partner finds something on his ass, he's gonna be state property alright."

Smoke was getting restless, and he wished the sarcastic police would hurry up so they could get Damu. He glanced in the squad-car and noticed the mounted AR-15.

"That's a nice piece of machinery you got their officer."

"Yeah, that's a AR-15. They were issued to us in 1996 when those two maniac bank robbers discharged over a thousand rounds at us. Now we've evened things up just in case some more assholes wanna try it again."

Smoke glanced up the street and suddenly became fixated on what he saw. The large black police officer was placing handcuffs on Kay, while the other black officer kicked Fatts up the ass and pointed in the opposite direction, demanding him to walk.

Fatts wobbled off with his head down displaying slight traces of embarrassment as Kay submitted to the officer's arrest. Smoke instantly became puzzled when he saw the other officer sit the empty duffle bag on top of the camero during his thorough search. He glanced back over to Damu, and his heart began to flutter as he watched Damu and his boys climb back in the hummer and pull off.

The officers poked around for another five minutes, then left... Smoke pulled off in a hurry. He rode pass the parked camero and caught up with Fatts.

He jumped out and trotted up to him.

"Whuddup dawg, what da' fuck just happened back there?"

"Man they took my brother to jail for a few different things. He owed tickets, had a misdemeanor warrant. And his license was expired."

Smoke took a second to let it register before responding.

"What about da' work, what happened?"

Fatts displayed a wide goofy grin as he pulled his shirt and stomach up revealing the neatly placed drugs in a black strap-on device with multiple large pockets attached. Smoke quickly snatched his shirt back down in hopes that Ray Ray didn't see it. He mentally noted that it was brilliant the way all those bulky drugs laid so orderly between the gross rows of fat.

"Dawg, get in so I can hurry up and see if that nigga Damu is still in the vicinity." Fatts quickly got in the back seat and Smoke pulled off......

After searching the area for thirty minutes with no luck, they decided to go back to Kay's house....

Fatts went in to put the drugs up, and when he returned, he joined in with Smoke and Ray Ray as they brainstormed about the earlier events.

"Damn dawg, them bitch-ass cops jacked off that opportunity." Smoke complained.

"Now it ain't no tellin when we gon' see him again."

Ray Ray interjected.

"Fatts, go in the crib and get them mac-tens that the police didn't find so we can finish lookin' for that sucka."

"What mac te- "

"Naw dawg!" Smoke nervously cut Fatts off.

"Don't worry about it, we'a go get our own heat 'cause yo' brother might have somethin' specific planned with those." Ray Ray glanced at Smoke with a funny expression as he thought to himself, *This nigga think I'm stupid, and that I didn't peep the lil drug deal he put down. That's the last time he gon' play me like that. Next time I'mma treat'em like a stranger."*

Smoke spoke up again when the tension subsided.

"Man, that lil freak Damu was talkin' to was a lil cutie."

"Yeah, she a tight lil thang. I know her, her name Shae."

Smoke reacted excitedly.

"Fatts, you know her?"

"Yeah cuz, My brother paid her to give me some head one day, and the bitch vomited all over my dick. I was mad as hell."

"Damn Fatts, what caused the bitch to throw-up on yo' shit?"

"Cuz, dat bitch talkin' 'bout she ain't never sucked a fat boy dick befoe, and that I had a odor to me. Cuz I ain't have no odor, it's just that I farted while she was gobblin' me up."

Smoke and Fatts exploded in laughter.

"Damn dawg, you'a silly muhfucka, fo'real. But check this out, can you get in contact with her again?"

"Yeah, I still got her number."

"Well call that bitch and see if you can persuade her to come get some moe' poot dick." Fatts laughed as he went to get her number. When he returned, he dialed the number on his cellphone and waited for an answer.

"Hello."

"Uh, is this Shae?"

"Yeah this Shae, who is this?"

"This Fatts baby, remember me?"

Shae paused for a moment as she tried to recollect where she knew him from.

"Are you talkin bout Kay loke's brother?"

"Yeah, that's me baby."

"Well whatchu want, Fatts?"

"I want the same thang I wanted the last time I saw you."

"Nigga please! I ain't into fat boys no'moe."

Fatts covered the phone for a moment while he laughed, then quickly regained his composure.

"You mean to tell me you ain't into money nomoe."

"Hell yeah I'm into money, but it'a damn sho' be much more than you spent last time."

Smoke smiled as he held his ear close to Fatts phone, listening to her conversation with him.

"Well how much money you talkin' 'bout Shae? 'cause last time Kay gave you five hundred."

"Well this time you gon' triple that."

"Hell na-," Smoke quickly covered the mouthpiece on the phone.

"Dawg, tell her you got that."

"Man she talkin' 'bout fifteen hundred for a punk ass head job, fuck that."

"Dawg, I got the bill, now tell'er."

Fatts displayed a rebellious expression before responding.

"Check this out Shae, I got that for ya, so whassup baby. Show me you about 'dat paper."

"A'ight Fatts, I'm down. And I don't want no bullshit outta you when it's time to kick out my paper. Matter fact, I want half as soon as I step out the car, bet?"

"Bet girl, now come on over. You remember where I stay at, right?"

"Yeah I remember. I'll be thru in ten minutes. Holla."

. . . .

CHAPTER 7

The moment Shae stepped out of her gray E-320 benz that her friend pulled back off in, Fatts looked her up and down. He marveled at the way her tight gray Dolce and Gabana shorts wrapped around her thick thighs and revealed the full print of her pussy. And how her jet-black skin seemed to have no flaws. Her perky breasts sat at full attention as her semi-hard nipples protruded through the short halter top she wore. Her unblemished toes peeked out through the gray square-heeled sandals, and they were painted burgundy like the dye in her popcorn-braided hair. When she smiled, revealing her pearly whites, Fatts thought to himself, *"this bitch so goddamn fine that she need to be farted on again."*

"Whuddup Shae. Here you go baby, half, just like we agreed."

Shae put the money in her purse and followed Fatts in the house. He didn't waste any time taking her in the bedroom. He pulled off his shirt and stepped out of his pants and boxers, then sat on the bed. Shae almost slipped and let Fatts see the frown that she was trying to conceal at the sight of his fleshy overweight body. She quickly pulled a half-pint of Jack Daniel's from her purse and took three large swallows from it.

Fatts reached under his stomach and played with himself until he had a semi-erection, then Shae took a deep breath, got on her knees, and began to suck him off. She couldn't imagine being sensuous with him, so she just sucked him in a steady rhythm trying to make him cum as quickly as possible. It was hard for her to concentrate because the smell from their first encounter still lingered in her mind. She couldn't wait for it to be over, and his heavy breathing annoyed her to the point where she wanted to gag him with something to shut him up.

"Shae, this demonstration feels good, but you need to be tryin' to swallow a little more of this dick if you want the other half of yo money."

Shae was about to stop and go berserk on his fat ass, but she decided to respect the fact that he peeped her game, and that it was time to suck it like she meant it. Suddenly, Fatts let out a sissified moan as she swallowed the entire length of him. She began to deep-throat him with a new degree of suction, and he squirmed and moved as if he was trying to get away. She didn't let up because she knew he would surely bust off quick now. She suddenly felt disgusted as the moisture from the bottom of his stomach excreted on to her forehead, but she kept steady with her new rhythm.

"Oow, ah, aha, damn Shae, ah. That's what I-I'm talkin' 'bout. I'm bout to- ah, ah, aaah," pffst! Baaaaaaaaaaaarrrrrnnt! Fatts let out a loud fart as he came in her mouth. And the smell was instantly in the air.

"You fat nasty muthafucka! Gimee my money so I can get the fuck up outta' here."

Fatts sat on the bed and chuckled as his dick slowly disappeared back into his stomach. He gave her the rest of the money, then asked,

"When we gon' get together again Shae?"

"Wheneva' you ready to spend a million fuckin' dolla's nigga! 'cause that's exactly how much you betta' have if you dial my number again, and not a penny less."

Shae stormed out the room headed for the front door but was quickly stopped by Smoke and Ray Ray.

"Hold up a minute baby, let me and my dawg holla atchu about somethin." Shae stepped back aggressively.

"Hold up potna, I hope yall muhfucka's ain't 'bout to start no funny shit, 'cause I ain't wit it." Shae sassed at Smoke.

"Naw baby, ain't no funny shit jumpin' off with us, we just think you could help us get intouch with a mutual friend."

"And what mutual friend is that?"

"His name is Damu."

"Damu, what makes you think I can help yall get intouch with Damu?"

"Because we know you associate with him."

"What you mean associate with him, I just met that nigga today."

"Well that's a start," said Smoke sarcastically.

"Now check this out baby, I'm already hip to how you roll, therefore, I'm willing to put my money where my mouth is." He exposed a thick wad of money and pilled off fifteen-hundred and handed it to her.

"Now I'ma give you fifteen-hundred more after you go out on a date with him and let me barge in on yall so I can take some pictures of you and him together. I'm tryna put a blackmail game down on him with another lil chick that he call wifey. So after I get the pictures of yall, you'a get yo money, and we go our separate ways. Cool?" He concluded his statement with open hands.

Shae stayed quiet with a *'Yeah Right'* expression for

about two full minutes before commenting on the situation.

"Nigga please, pictures my ass. Where and when do you think I was born. Yesterday on planet silly. I know the shit is deeper than that, and I don't give a fuck what yall wanna do to the nigga 'cause I don't really know dude like that noway. But if my assumption is correct, it's gonna cost a little more than those figures you just threw out there. So whassup?"

Smoke smirked at her spunkiness before responding.

"A'ight Ms. Witty. Now that we have a better understanding of each other, how does five G's sound?"

"It sound like Damu is a nigga that's 'bout to come up short." Shae answered with glee in her eyes.

"A'ight then, cool. Now check this out. When do he wanna hook up with you?"

"Tomorrow," answered Shae.

"Did he leave you a phone number?"

"Naw, I gave him mines and he told me he'd call me around seven P.M."

"Okay, that's when we gon' put everything in motion," said Smoke as they concluded their discussion.

Fatts walked out the bedroom fully dressed now.

"Shae, you want me to run you to the crib, or you gon' call yo' girl to bring yo' ride?"

"You can drop me off 'cause I told my girl I would get myself home. And nigga don't be doin' none of that nasty-ass fartin-n-shit or I'll walk."

They all bust out laughin, then loaded up in the black Lincoln.

Fatts drove and Shae sat on the passenger side while Smoke and Ray Ray sat in the back seat.

"Ay Fatts, swing by yo' brother's Camero so we can take

it back to yall crib before that muhfucka get stripped, a'ight."

"Yeah Yeah-a'ight Smoke." Fatts answered annoyingly as he tried to give his undivided attention to the Jay-Z Blueprint cd that he had bumpin through the Bose system. He rocked his head hard, and accurately sung along with the words out loud.

"I can't see'em comin down my eyes, so I had to make the song cry." "Boy this my shit! This nigga be spittin' dat fire cuz." There was excitement in his tone.

"Boy cut that old shit off and put on some E-40 up in this muhfucka." Shae squawked as she pulled a E-40 cd out of her purse.

"Girl I fuck wit' my nigga 40 too, but we'a bump that later, I'm rockin' Jigga right now. And for yo' information, Jigga music don't never get old, so I'ma be rockin' his shit in two thousand fifty. Please believe it." Shae smacked her lips, then eagerly turned toward him.

"You just mad 'cause them lil lyrics you be tryna spit ain't fuckin' wit' E-40's.

Fatts got hyped up from her truthful remark, so he quickly popped back.

"Yeah, that may be true, but I ain't spittin' my own lyrics, I'm spittin' jigga lyrics. And I betcha' 40 wouldn't give yo' bucket-head ass the time of day."

"Nigga fuck you. And just because I like his music don't mean I'm tryna fuck."

"Yeah whateva, now shut the hell up and soak this game up that Jigga spittin' to yo'ass!"

Ray Ray and Smoke just laughed at the bickering.

They pulled up at the Camero five minutes later.

"Whatchu wanna do Fatts, you wanna take yo' brother's ride back to the crib, or you want us to take it while you drop her off?"

"Yall can gon' take it back Smoke, 'cause them lil bucket seats be killin' my big ass. Here go the keys." Smoke snatched the keys from the air.

"A'ight, we'a holla Fatts."

Smoke mashed the gas a few times and listened to the roar of the powerful hyped-up engine that Kay had under the hood.

"Damn dawg, this muhfucka's a road runner forreal."

Broom! Broom! Broom! -skirrrt! The Camero leaped forward into traffic as he slammed it in drive, then quickly came to a sudden halt behind Fatts as the red light caught them both.

"Dawg, who Shae remind you of?" Smoke asked out of the blue. Ray Ray immediately shook his head as if to say, *"Why you make me think about that bitch Syann."* Smoke smiled at his reaction before elaborating.

"Man, that bitch got all the potential of Syann, don't she?"

Ray Ray glanced out the window, appearing to be in deep thought before answering.

"Yeah dawg, I guess it's one in every hood."

The light turned green, and Fatts kept straight as Smoke paused in the intersection with his left blinker on.

"That fat muthafucka gon' try to get some more of that head from Shae before they make it to her crib, watch." Smoke joked as he waited for a break in the oncoming traffic to make his left turn... Suddenly, he noticed the brake lights on the Lincoln illuminate, as the ready-mix concrete truck in front of Fatts came to a sudden stop, all to avoid a collision with the 1964 red Impala that halted in front of it abruptly.

A few seconds later,

"Aw shit!" shouted Smoke, as two masked gunmen ran full speed towards the Lincoln. They held automatic handguns tight in their grip and didn't appear to be intimidated in the least bit. They both wore black kaki's, red-n-black plad shirts, and red with white-trim, Chuck Taylor Converse. And before anyone could fully peep what was really going on, they both simultaneously open fired on the Lincoln.

Shae screamed and tried to exit the car as the bullets riddled Fatts relentlessly. The shooters unexpectedly ceased fire for a moment, as if they realized the people in the car were'nt the intended targets. But a few moments later, they resumed the mission and open fired again, this time sending more bullets into Fatts while he threw his arm up in an effort to block the flying slugs. Fatts was so big, that his body effortlessly shielded most of the bullets from Shae as she constantly screamed and fumbled with the door handle.

She finally got the door open. And just as she was climbing out, two bullets caught her in the back of the head within seconds apart, leaving her upper body sprawled outside the car, with her legs still hanging inside. One of the shooters startlingly turned and open fired at the oncoming car, but it was too late as the high speed Camero made contact, sending his body flying into the back of the concrete truck. Ray Ray didn't waste any time jumping out going for the loose gun. Bullets barely missed him as the other shooter fired straight shots in his direction. Ray Ray dove and came up with the gun, then ducked behind the truck to shield himself from the multiple bullets.

Smoke quickly backed the Camero up, which caused the remaining shooter to start firing in his direction. He ducked as the bullets hit the windshield and shattered the passenger window...

Ray Ray took advantage of the opportunity and spun from behind the truck pumping several rounds into the shooter until his body dropped flagrantly... Ray Ray briskly crept his way over to the disabled gunman, and the moment he noticed the slightest movement, he coldly pumped two more rounds point-blank in his chest. The gunman's body jolted, and heaved upward from the ground, breathing what would be his last breath, then slowly descended back down to the concrete.

Ray Ray looked at Smoke to see if he was alright, and once Smoke confirmed it with a nod of his head, Ray Ray bent down and removed the ski mask from the deceased shooter.

"Whut 'da fuck!" he mumbled to himself when he noticed the shooter was a female. He didn't know her, but she was extremely familiar to him. He quickly ran over to the other deceased shooter and removed the ski mask. It was then that he knew exactly where he knew her from.

"Ay Smoke, this dat lil ruthless bitch Damiesha, and that's her girlfriend over there."

Smoke flashed a surprised expression, then shook it off and darted over to Shae's body and grabbed her cellphone from her purse.

"Come on Ray Ray, let's get da' fuck up outta here before them folks come."

They jumped in the camero and burned rubber leaving the scene.......

****

When they made it to one of their safe spots, they quickly devised a plan that would allow them to still make contact with Damu. Smoke picked up a loyal female friend named Doll on the way, to sit with them until Damu called Shae's phone. Smoke instructed Doll on what she would say when Damu called, and they just hoped he'd fall for it. Smoke lit up a blunt of cush and made small talk as they waited for the call, while Doll ate potatoe chips and sipped on a Heineken because she didn't smoke weed.

"Dawg, that lil bitch Damiesha remembered what the Lincoln looked like, and she was really tryna' kill us Smoke."

"Yeah I know, and I also know that Kay is gonna trip the fuck out when he find out his lil brother bit the dust.

Smoke instinctively glanced at Doll as she walked toward the bathroom. He admired how her tight figure complimented the apple-bottom jeans she wore, and the way she had her hair dyed black and brown only highlighted her smooth French vanilla skin complexion. Smoke rubbed his chin and wondered to himself why he'd never sexed her. But after a few moments of thought, he reflected on something a convict in the joint once said to him, *"Man, you can't fuck every chick you cool with, especially if you call her your friend. Sex and true friendship don't mix. It's a guaranteed recipe for drama that nine times outta ten, you ain't ready for. Take it from a old-head like myself, who been around the block a few times and is speakin from experience. My wife use to be my best friend before she was my wife. Now she just my wife because I can't get genuine dialogue from her anymore. Most of her feedback is saturated with fuckin emotions. So, in a nutshell, be smart fella."* Smoke smirked as he ended his thoughts.

"Doll." Smoke called out in a hurry as Shae's phone rung. He met her halfway with it in his hand, then gave her a look that indicated, *"don't mess this up."*

"Hello." She answered.,

"Can I speak to Shae?"

"This is Shae."

"Whuddup Shae, do you know who this is?"

"No, and I really don't feel like playin' no guessin' games."

"Well if you play just this once, it might be worth ya' while."

"Well okay, since you put it like that, it must be Denzel."

"Nope."

"Well how 'bout Morris Chestnut?"

"Wrong again, but I got good news for you. I'm better lookin' than both of those dudes."

"Well spare me the agony baby and reveal the man of my dreams to me."

Smoke and Ray Ray covered their mouths as they laughed at how good she imitated Shae from nothing but the information they provided her with.

"This Damu baby."

"Damu, Damu who?"

"Oh, you forgot me already?"

"Naw baby I'm just playin. I knew who you was from jump."

"How is that?"

"Because you said you'd call at a specific time, and right now is that specific time. And I figured you was a man of your word, so I figured it was you. And what'll ya' know, I was right."

"You sound a little different Shae."

"Is that right? Well that's because I got my teeth cleaned today, and that shit be havin' me sounding funny afterwards. I was hopin' you didn't notice."

"Well it's hard not to notice every little thing about you. Know what I'm sayin. Anyway, can you fall thru?"

"Yeah, I can, and I'd rather you come get me, it's more lady like."

"Well baby, I promise to treat you like nothin' less than a lady when you get here, but I won't be able to come swoop you because I'm watching over something very important, and I can't leave right now. Catch a cab if yo' car ain't available, I'll pay for it."

Doll pouted outloud for a moment before giving in to his request.

"Alright, but you don't gotta' pay for my cab fare, I got it."

"Don't play me like that Shae, I got it."

"Well alright, but the next time we date, you will be comin' to get me, is that understood?"

"Yeah, whateva' you say Shae." Damu gave her the address then hung up....

Smoke could tell that Damu hadn't heard about Damiesha's death yet. And he desperately wanted to get to him before he did....

CHAPTER 8

When Damu noticed the cab parked in front of his hideout, he knew it could only be one person, so he hurried out the front door and walked up to the cab. His eyes squinted and a frown appeared on his face when Doll stepped out.

"Who da' fuck is you?"

"Your dream girl."

"Bitch where Shae at?"

"Right here nigga!" Smoke snarled as he pressed the ten shot 45 to the back of his head.

"Walk nigga," Smoke demanded as Doll pulled back off in the cab. Smoke and Ray Ray calmly scanned the area as they walked Damu up to his front door.

"Open the door nigga, and don't try no funny shit."

When Damu opened the door, four of his gang members yelled out,

"Comeer Bitch!" simultaneously as they all stood there naked holding their dicks. They expected to see Shae but was shocked when they saw Smoke and Ray Ray instead. They quickly scrambled to get their clothes and guns but was immediately subdued by Ray Ray.

They all laid face down naked, and Ray Ray slowly made his way to each of them applying duct tape to their hands and mouth... As they all sat there wondering what was next to come, a breaking news story about

Damiesha's death flashed across the television. Smoke impolitely turned off the tv, then moments later, he noticed Damu's facial expression transform into a man of pure rage. He suddenly lunged out the chair at Smoke and charged at him aggressively... Boh! "Aaaahhhgg!" Damu dropped to the floor clutching his leg as Ray Ray let off the quick shot to his left thigh... When Damu saw the report about his little sister, it enraged him, and he instinctively reacted. ...Smoke harshly lifted him up and sat him back in the chair.

"Now sit yo' ass there and bleed nigga, and if you try that dumb shit again, I'ma put a muhfuckin hole the size of a grapefruit in yo' big ass head." Smoke snarled. Ray Ray tossed Smoke the duct tape, and he didn't waste any time taping his body to the chair.

After everybody was securely bound, Ray Ray searched the house thoroughly for his babies. But all he found was nearly two-hundred thousand in cash, six kilos of cocaine and several automatic weapons. He bagged up the money and left the coke and a few weapons where it was, then walked back in the living room to begin his interrogation on Damu.

"A'ight you bitch-ass nigga, I didn't come here to play with you. Where da' fuck is my babies at?"

Damu didn't respond, he just sat there trying to get use to the pain that the bullet caused. Ray Ray quickly slapped blood from his mouth with the pistol.

"Where da' fuck is my babies' man?" he asked again as he felt his anger building up, but Damu still didn't answer.

Smoke stepped in and grabbed him by the shirt and got close to his face.

"Check this out dawg, you gon' talk whether you want

to or not. And like you told me, it ain't a threat, it's a promise. Now where the fuck is the kid's nigga?" Damu looked up slowly and asked, "What kids' nigga?" Clack! Ray Ray slapped him with the gun again then yelled to the top of his lungs,

"Where my babies at muthafucka!"

Damu spit blood from his mouth before calmly responding,

"What kids?" Ray Ray quickly aimed the gun at his head, but Smoke grabbed it just as quickly.

"Naw Ray Ray! We need this bitch alive. But trust me, you know I can think of a million and one things that we can do to make this nigga wish he was dead. And I'ma make it go on and on 'til he tell us where the babies at. When it rains it pours nigga, remember?"

Ray Ray quickly ran outside to the black Impala they drove and grabbed a sledgehammer from the trunk. When he walked through the door, Smoke immediately started laughin.

"That's right dawg, let's take it back to the old school and tap that nigga's knee caps with that sledge drama."

Ray Ray stepped closer to Damu.

"Dawg, is you ready to stop bullshitten and tell me where my babies at?" Damu slowly lifted his head and strained to form a bloody smile in his nauseous state.

"Is you talkin 'bout the ones with the missing heads?" Damu began laughing at his own sarcastic statement, and Ray Ray became infuriated. His face motioned upward, and his eyes became aglow as he wound the sledgehammer one good time and slammed it down as hard as he could on Damu's right knee-cap.

Damu released a piercing shriek that sounded inhuman as the heavy piece of steel shattered his knee, causing the biggest bone to burst through the skin and stick outside of his leg. A few seconds later, he passed out from the unbearable pain, and Ray Ray stood over him breathing like a maniac.

"Damn," whispered Smoke as his cell phone rung.

"Hello," he answered, then spoke into the receiver for about five minutes, then hung up.

"Dawg, that was Kay. He made bond and he want me to come scoop him up, so I'll be right back." Smoke left, and Ray Ray searched the house for more clues to his daughters' whereabouts.

He became frustrated when he found nothing, so he decided to interrogate the four gang members on the floor. By the time Smoke showed back up with Kay-loc, Ray Ray was interrogating the last dude.

"Man, I don't know nothing about no babies, fo'real. Damu is the homie, and we all know that he can get a little extreme from time to time, but we ain't into everything that he into, straight up blood." Ray Ray was tired of all the bullshit and didn't know how much more he could take before he went off the deep end.

Kay immediately ran up to Damu and slapped his unconscious face the moment he walked through the door.

"Whussup now you bitch-ass nigga!" He ran over to the other four dudes on the floor and began kicking and stomping them in the face.

"Cuz let me get yo' heater so I can off these niggas cuz! These bitches killed four of my soldiers, and then turn around and killed my baby brother! Gimee the heat Smoke, it's over for these hoes."

Smoke didn't give an immediate response, he just stared at Kay because he knew what was going through his head. Kay wasn't only vexed about the recent losses he took, but it was the overall losses he took amongst his crew that drove a dagger in his heart, especially Fatts. And although gang-bangin' was a major part of his livelihood, it was still painful to know that things like deceased baby brothers could never be replaced. Kay felt that his predicament was truly a sign of bad karma because he sincerely had stopped bangin' in his heart a long time ago. His primary focus was mostly about gettin' fast-money and taking care of family. And the only reason he continued to bang actively, was basically to maintain respect among his homies, and enemies alike. After hesitating for a few moments, Smoke softly mumbled,

"Fuck it," then stepped forward and handed Kay the gun.

A wave of muffled pleas could immediately be heard through the duct-taped mouths of the captives on the floor, all except the one who's tape was left off his mouth after Ray Ray interrogated him. He babbled about answering a phone as Kay eagerly accepted the gun from Smoke... When Kay walked over to the line of men and aimed the gun at them, the free-mouthed gang member frantically yelled,

"Hold up blood! Listen! You need to answer that phone, seriously!"

"Whut phone nigga?" asked Kay.

"The phone that's ringing in Damu's pocket blood, he got two phones, and there's only one person on the planet that calls that phone. So you need to answer it blood. Now!"

As everyone settled down for a moment, they suddenly could actually hear a ringing phone. Ray Ray walked over to Damu's slumped-over body and reached in his pocket and got the phone. He glanced around at everybody momentarily before answering it, then pressed the button,

"Hello."

"One time deep!" said the caller then hung up.

Ray Ray glanced around the room again with a confused expression before speaking.

"Whut they say blood?" the man on the floor asked eagerly as he strained his neck in an effort to look back at Ray Ray.

"They said one time deep."

"Blood! If yall don't wanna go to jail, yall betta' get the fuck up outta' here like now! That was our warning."

"Cuz I think he bluffin," shouted Kay.

"I'm tellin you blo-, clack! "Now say blood outch'o mouth one mo' time and I'ma kill you faster than you already scheduled to die nigga."

After the pain subsided from the quick blow Kay delivered with the gun, the man frowned as the blood ran down the side of his face then continued his statement.

"Man Damu got a inside plug with the police, and dude ain't failed us yet, they comin' right now!"

Kay glanced at Smoke.

"Ay Smoke, walk out on the porch and tell me if you see anything cuz. And if you don't, I'm killin' these niggas as soon as you walk back in."

Smoke smiled and replied,

"I'm down wit that," then casually walked outside. He looked up the street to his left for about sixty seconds. Then slowly turned and looked up the street to his right. He didn't see any police so he shrugged it off, then headed back toward the front door.

Just as he reached for the doorknob, he glanced to his

left once more off instinct,

"Oh shit!" he shouted when he saw the raid-van with several unmarked cars from the LAPD narcotics division, converging on the house... Smoke rushed through the door with panic in his demeanor.

"Let's ride! Let's ride! He wasn't lyin dawg! Let's get the fuck up outta' here." Ray Ray instantly cut the tape from Damu and slung him over his shoulder. He pointed at the bag of money and instructed Smoke to retrieve it.

They went out the back door and made it a few blocks over to the backup car that they parked just in case things got ugly. And it came in handy as they made it out of the vicinity undetected by the law. The police had been tipped off about the weight that Damu's gang was selling out of the house. They took all four gang members to jail after finding the cocaine, along with the multiple automatic weapons. Most of the money and coke that was there in the beginning, belonged to some blood gang members from Kansas City, that Damu had robbed a few days prior to the raid. Damu hated other bloods from out of state. He would refer to them as counterfeit thugs. He barely respected other blood-sets from LA. But it disgusted him to see people from anywhere else claim blood, because he felt they were phony, and wasn't creative enough to come up with their own sets.

Later on that night, Ray Ray sat in a chair across from Damu, watching and listening as he came in and out of consciousness. He wondered what he would do if his babies were already deceased. He knew it would destroy Sheila mentally, and that their marriage and life together would never be the same.

He slowly walked over to Damu and waved some smelling salt a few inches under his nostrils, then watched as he flinched from the strong vapors that it released. He opened his eyes and smiled when he saw Ray Ray.

"What the fuck you smilin' about nigga?"

"I'm smilin' at you blood. I'm just trippin' about-ahh!" Damu dropped his head and closed his eyes tight as the pain from his leg kicked in before he continued.

"I'm trippin about the fact that you didn't kill me yet. You must be one of them –ahh!- soft niggas."

Ray Ray smirked before responding.

"You know as well as I do, that yo' bitch-ass woulda' been dead a long time ago if it wasn't for my babies. Now I'm tired of playin' games with yo' punk-ass. Tell me where my babies at, then you can go back to yo' fucked-up life, and I can go back to mine."

Damu smiled again, then suddenly sent a spray of spit towards Ray Ray's face. Ray Ray dodged most of it, then angrily pulled out his gun and slapped him across the bridge of his nose, breaking it instantly. He then put the nine to the exposed bone that protruded from Damu's wounded leg and applied pressure to it as if he was trying to push it back in place.

"Aaaaahhhhhhhggg!" Damu screamed out in pain as the cold steel from the barretta shifted the bone against the discarded flesh.

Ray Ray removed it a few seconds later, then demanded answers again.

"Dawg, I think you betta' start talkin, 'cause you lookin' like a real lil bitch right now. Now where da' fuck is my babies?"

Damu breathed heavily and sweated profusely as he tried to catch his breath. He was weak from the significant loss of blood, as well as all the straining he was doing to keep from submitting to the agonizing pain. He sat there with a tight-faced expression from the pain and didn't say a word.

Ray Ray instantly applied pressure again to counter his stubbornness, but this time he pressed much harder than he did before.

"Aaaaaahhhhgg! Aaaaaahhhh!" Damu screamed out again as the razor-sharp pains dominated his body. He was more than ready for it to stop but stopping wasn't an option with Ray Ray until he suddenly noticed Damu's eyes began to roll in the back of his head. He didn't want Damu to pass out again, so he pulled back. Damu dropped his head forward after nearly fainting. He was completely exhausted from the abuse. He remained fixed in that position for ten minutes, then suddenly mumbled to Ray Ray through clutched teeth.

"Alright blood, I'll tell you where they at."

Ray Ray sat there and listened to the information attentively for ten minutes, then anxiously stormed out the door with Smoke and Kay on his heels. They drove over the speed limit and made it to the location that Damu gave them in twenty minutes.

Ray Ray re-checked the address on the small piece of paper to confirm that they were at the correct house, then glanced around at Kay and Smoke as if he really didn't want to go in.

The house was definitely abandoned, and Ray Ray tried everything in his power to prepare himself mentally to see his babies in whatever condition they were in, as long as they were alive. He took a deep breath, then slowly walked in. A bad odor lingered throughout the house, but Ray Ray didn't panic because he was familiar with it. It was the smell of dead rats and rotten food.

They all separated and searched the house individually, and Ray Ray began calling out to them as he searched.

"Myonly! Love! Say something babies if yall hear me, daddy's here, and I came to take yall home." Ray Ray continued to call out to them as they searched room after room.

Suddenly, Ray Ray heard a muffled scream from what sounded like Smoke, so he didn't waste any time making it to where he was.

Smoke was scurrying away from the room as Ray Ray was walking up. They both stopped in front of each other, and Ray Ray immediately spoke up.

"You a'ight man?" Smoke's face displayed a mixture of discombobulation and fear. And he didn't answer Ray Ray's question, he just grabbed him by the arm and pulled him in the opposite direction.

"Come on Ray Ray, let's search the rest of the rooms, and if they don't turn up, we'a just kill dat nigga when we get back."

"Hold up Smoke, slow down dawg, you still ain't answered my question. And what da' hell was you screamin' about?"

"I saw a big ass rat. And you know I hate rats." Smoke spoke convincingly, but Ray Ray wasn't buyin' it.

He knew Smoke like a book and saw straight through his lies. He snatched away from Smoke aggressively, then headed toward the room Smoke had just left… Smoke quickly jumped in front of him with a more frightening look on his face now.

"Ray Ray, please man, let's keep searchin."

Ray Ray knew that whatever was responsible for Smoke's strange behavior was behind that door. He stared at Smoke so hard, that the energy from his eyes was enough to pierce his soul.

"Move dawg." Ray Ray demanded in a low snarl.

Smoke stood there a few seconds longer, until the silent life or death understanding registered in his mind. He was fully aware of the fact that Ray Ray wasn't going to ask him to move again. The cocked pistol in Ray Ray's hand helped Smoke quickly come up with that assumption, so he submissively stepped to the side and let him pass...

Ray Ray paused for a moment after he twisted the doorknob. He took a deep breath...looked up toward the ceiling...then pushed the door open...

When his mind projected what his eyes saw, his mouth dropped open and his heart went berserk.... He attempted to scream, but nothing came out... He backed into the wall and slid down to the floor as the steady stream of tears fell from his eyes...

His worst fears were now a reality as he witnessed the two tiny skulls that sat side by side on an old wooden table. He realized that this was Damu's signature trademark whenever he snatched somebody's kids. It was the ultimate way of saying, *"his wars will be fought without mercy, so the enemy should never expect any."* It almost seemed satanic in a sense. And it definitely let the opposition know that morals were long gone from Damu, if there ever was any in him in the first place. Ray Ray couldn't believe his babies were gone forever, and he truly didn't know how he would go on without them. He sat on the floor and wept for a few more minutes, then stood up slow with hate in his heart and vengeance on his mind.

He stormed pass Smoke and Kay headed for the car and drove like a madman getting back to Damu.... Fifteen minutes later, Ray Ray rushed through the front door of the safe spot where Damu was held captive. His blood boiled as he approached him with lighting speed delivering a barrage of punches to his already busted up face. Damu took the punches as best as he could, then attempted to smile because he understood what the sudden attack was about. He knew that they'd found the children's remains, and the pain in his body was so unbearable that he hoped and anticipated a sudden death.

He quickly braced himself and smiled again when it seemed like his wish was about to be granted, as Ray Ray eagerly pressed the 45 to the side of his temple.

Damu knew by now that Ray Ray was just as thorough as him, so he felt a sense of relief just knowing the weapon would be discharged at any moment... And the bullet would travel through his skull and put him out of his misery.

"Boh!" was all he heard when Ray Ray pulled the trigger. He remained silent for a moment, awaiting his arrival to hell. 'Cause heaven was ruled out a long time ago.

After approximately 30 seconds of silence, he suddenly became slightly confused. He thought, *"pain and memory was supposed to go away in death."* He wondered why he still felt discomfort and still possessed rational thoughts.

"Damn." He mumbled to himself. *"Maybe it takes a minute before it all goes away. Or maybe I didn't die instantly.*

I wish the process would speed up 'cause this shit ain't cool." Suddenly, he heard a familiar voice.

"You ain't dead yet you bitch ass nigga!" Ray Ray snarled.

"Did you think I was gon' let you off that easy?"

Clack!

Ray Ray slapped him across the face with the gun, then

placed it on the table and picked up the sledgehammer. He displayed the expression of a maniac as he walked back toward Damu. His eyes were bucked, and tears seemed to be entwined in what appeared to be foam in the corners of his mouth.

He swung the sledgehammer in a whipping half of circle and brought it down with all his might on Damu's other leg. Damu's screams could be heard throughout the house and several blocks away. Ray Ray swung again and broke Damu's right shoulder. Then he broke his left collar bone. And as Damu fell out the chair, the sound of another cracking bone could instantly be heard as the sledgehammer landed on him again. Ray Ray stood over him as he moaned and squirmed on the floor. He watched unremorsefully as Damu begged for mercy in body language. Ray Ray's anger suddenly grew beyond comprehension as he thought about the torture his babies must've endured, then he savagely slammed the sledgehammer into Damu's face. He swung again... then swung again... then swung again as if he was chopping wood with an ax. Damu's head and face was now unrecognizable as the blood and brains oozed out freely.

Ray Ray continued to swing until he was so exhausted that he could barely lift the sledgehammer anymore...

When it was finally over, Damu laid dead. And the sight of his corpse was gruesome in every way. His legs and arms looked as if they were made of silly puddy, and parts of his skull was embedded into the wooden floor.

Ray Ray stayed transfixed on the bludgeoned body for a suspended fifteen minutes, then slowly walked away.

He left the house without saying a word to Smoke or Kay. And during his ride home, he thought of a million ways to break the news to Sheila, but none of them seemed to be good enough. His world had crumbled all over again, and just knowing he had to witness Sheila crumble, only made his agony that much greater....

****

Ray Ray strolled through the house avoiding Sheila as long as he could, but his running came to an end when Sheila unexpectedly stepped in front of him, blocking his path as he exited the bathroom.

"Ray Ray, is there something you want to tell me?"

Her question totally caught Ray Ray off guard. And it stung his ears as he matched it with the distressful expression on her face. He knew he had to tell her, *but not now, why now.*

His thoughts took refuge, and he anxiously awaited them to return with the solution to his problem.

"What do I say? How do I say it? How do you tell a mother she'll never see her children again? Or do you just say it?"

His thoughts swarmed through his head like a pack of bees on the move. He stared at her for five eternal minutes before deciding, this was it. There was nowhere else to run too. He gently slid his hand into hers and escorted her to the bedroom. He sat her down, then reluctantly sat down beside her. He cleared his throat, then let out a heavy sigh.

"Sheila, I want you to listen, and listen carefully."

Sheila's hands began to tremble, and her nose perspired as she braced herself for a worse-case scenario.

"Sheila,"- riiinng! His sentence was interrupted from his ringing cell phone. His first instinct was to ignore it, but when he second-guessed it, he thought, maybe he should answer it because at least it would buy him a little more time to prepare for the fixed heavyweight fight, in the form of Sheila that he was destined to lose.

"Hello." He answered.

"May I speak to Raynard Thompson, a-k-a Ray Ray?" Ray Ray hadn't heard anybody call him by his government name since his last encounter with the feds, so he immediately became defensive.

"You must have the wrong number guy." click. Ray Ray hung up. But before he could resume his conversation with Sheila, his cell phone rung again.

"Hello?"

"Ray Ray, it would be wise for you to not hang up again. Now I need you to give me your undivided attention and just listen 'til I'm done."

"Who da' fuck is this?" Ray Ray snarled.

"It's Myonly and Love, and if that's not enough to arouse your curiosity, you can blame whatever happens to them on ya'self after this phone call. Now you ready to listen or what?"

Ray Ray immediately walked to another room with the phone for some privacy from Sheila.

"Is this some kind of joke? My babies are already deceased."

"No they're not, but if you don't meet my demands, they will be."

"Well how do I know they're a-"

"If you would just shut the fuck up and listen like I told you to, I'll tell you how."

Ray Ray quickly told himself that this wasn't the time to challenge the bastard on the other end of the phone, especially if he was telling the truth about Myonly and Love, so he restrained his tongue from unleashing a spew of obscenities' and submitted to the conversation.

"Now listen, there's a fax machine service about a block away from LAX airport. I want you to go there in 30 minutes and go to the customer service window and tell them you're expecting a fax from Detroit, from a person name Jimmy, code name Hearts. And immediately after that, I want you to focus on nothing but the mission at hand. Now listen and listen well because I don't want you to miss any details."

Ray Ray stayed on the phone for fifteen more minutes, then hung up and dashed out the door. He called Smoke on the road and instructed him to meet him at the fax spot A.S.A.P.

Smoke pulled up five minutes after Ray Ray, and Ray Ray rushed up to him and handed him the faxed photograph of Myonly and Love that was taken 30 minutes ago. They were alive and well, and Ray Ray felt like a ton of pressure was lifted from his heart.

"So it wasn't Damu after all huh?" said Smoke.

"Naw, it wasn't. And I guess those two skulls that we found belonged to those other babies he snatched up." Ray Ray added.

"Well put me up on game, who is dude that got the babies?"

"Man, it's a Spanish muthafucka from the southwest side of Detroit name Deo. He talkin' 'bout I inherited my fathers debt to them when he died. He said my pops owed them a half a mil, and that it grew interest on it for every year that I didn't pay."

Smoke frowned before responding.

"So what is they sayin' the ticket is now?"

"Fifteen point one million."

"Whut!!" shouted Smoke.

"How in the fuck is a debt gon' go from half a mil to

15.1 mil?"

Ray Ray looked off in the distance before responding. And the print of his lower jawbone could be seen twitching as he reflected on the audacity of the kidnapper's.

"Dawg, it's just a classic case of street muthafucka's makin they own rules. You know how the game go Smoke.

Especially when somebody credible already put them up on our status. They probably wanted to press us a long time ago but they never had the leverage to do it until now... But check this out dawg, dude told me I got two weeks to come up with the bread or it was over for my babies. I can get my hands on five mil cash, but the rest of my shit is tied up in real-estate investments and different business venture's-n-shit." Ray Ray explained honestly.

"Well I can scrape up about six in cash by tomorrow and that's where my juice run out dawg."

"Damn dawg, that ain't enough. We gotta come up with four more before we make this trip to Detroit."

"Yeah I know Ray. And I also know it's gonna be real dangerous bein' in the D with all the heat we got on us."

"Well, that means we gotta be extra careful. But fuck that for now. My only concern is getting up on the rest of that change so I can get my babies back, then kill the muthafucka's who took'em. Do you know of any quick licks we can hit that would produce that kinda' change?"

Smoke hesitated for a few seconds with a smirky expression before answering Ray Ray's question. Then smiled, because just the mere thought of him pulling off a caper with Ray Ray after all these years, thrilled him.

"I thought you'd never ask baby. I got the perfect sucka in mind. It's a dude that be coppin' from me name Ceelo.

He moved out here from Battlecreek Michigan 'cause his money made him feel like he's a Hollywood type nigga. The lil nigga is caked up too. And his biggest mistake is that he always braggin' about his paper. And his dumbest mistake is that he give too many loose details on where to find it. He's one of the niggas that I always kept on the backburner for times like this. Now let's go get this chump so we can get yo' babies back."

Smoke smiled again as they jumped in the car.

"It's like old times baby."

Ray Ray shook his head with a slight smirk because he knew that Smoke was truly a thrill seeker.

CHAPTER 9

Myonly and Love awoke from their light sleep as the short Spanish man entered the room again. He casually placed another bag of McDonalds on the table, then grabbed the old untouched bags and put them in a large black garbage bag. He lit a cigarette then sat down in a chair.

"I think you young ladies would feel a lot better if you eat. Liquid's will keep you alive, but it's been over a week now, and your health is not gonna hold up much longer like this. Now eat up. Everybody likes McDonalds."

"I want my daddy!" shouted Love.

"And I'm sure your daddy wants you too. But if you don't eat, you'll let your daddy down because the next time he see's you, he won't see that same pretty smile that he's used to seeing on you. Now eat up."

Love sniffled a few times before blurting.

"Are you gonna hurt us?"

The man gave a short smirk, then stepped closer to her.

"Sweetheart, if I was gonna hurt you, I woulda' done it a long time ago."

"Well why do you wear that mask?" asked Love.

"Sweetheart, whenever your enemy where's a mask in a situation like this, consider it a good thing. Because it normally means he has an agenda that has to be fulfilled. And that once his agenda is fulfilled, he has intentions on letting you go live a normal life without fear of repercussions. Because he knows you haven't seen his face. You understand? Now I think we've done enough talking for today. Eat your food and play with the play station. There's at least twenty different games over there."

The man walked out and locked the door to the plush room behind him. Love thought about what the man had said about returning to her father safely, so she slowly opened the McDonalds bag and unwrapped one of the quarter pounders. She put it to Myonly's mouth first, but Myonly refused it.

"Come on Myonly, we gotta eat. We gotta stay strong so we can get back to daddy. Now eat." Love bit into the burger, then Myonly followed her lead and took a little bite.

"That's right sis, we gotta stay alive, 'cause if we don't, daddy's gonna be pissed.

CHAPTER 10

.... After Smoke and Ray Ray secured the 5.1 million in cash that Ceelo had stashed throughout the lavish mansion, Ceelo continued to plead with them to release his companion.

"Come on Smoke man, just let her go. She don't got nothing to do with my business affairs."

Smoke ignored him as he fixed himself a shot of Belvidere vodka from the full-size bar. He glanced over at Ceelo and laughed at how him and his companion squirmed from the duct tape that bound their hands together.

Ray Ray stared at Ceelo and got pissed because of the striking resemblance he had to Pooh. They had the same light complexion and the same hazel eyes. The only difference was, Pooh was much taller than him, and wasn't nearly as soft as this dude in character.

Smoke focused on Ceelo's companion because something puzzled him and made him constantly stare. At first, he thought it was the short skirt or the overall sleezy appearance. But after a few moments of observation, he instinctively got up and walked over to them. He unexpectedly reached down and snatched her panties down, which allowed a nine-inch dick to spring into view.

"Goddamn dawg!" smoke shouted, then briskly turned

to Ceelo. "Ay man, did you know you was layin' up here freakin' with a man?"

"Of course he knew, that's how he get down." Yelled the dark-complected homosexual.

"And why in the fuck did you snatch my wig and panties down muthafucka!" Smoke quickly delivered a hard kick to the punk's face for gettin' sassy, while Ray Ray laughed at Smoke's anger.

"Damn dawg, I didn't know you get down like that. With that gorgeous wife you got at the crib. Now I really don't feel bad about taxin' yo' bitch ass." Smoke berated Ceelo.

Ceelo acted as if none of what had just taken' place mattered. He still pitched his same plea.

"Smoke, just let her go man, she don't got nothin' to do with this, a'ight. Just do this for me man, please."

Smoke turned toward Ray Ray in amazement.

"You hear this punk muthafucka man. He straight up in love with dude, ha ha. And stop sayin 'she' nigga. He's a muthafuckin man. If you put lipstick on a pig, it's still a pig dude.

Ray Ray was tired of looking and listening to the whole situation... He spontaneously gave Smoke a look that meant *'playtime's over.'* Then casually pulled the ten millimeters from his waistband... Ray Ray approached the cross-dressed man and spoke matter-of-factly.

"Check this out dude, I'm not about to kill you because you gay. I'm not plagued by that term people use called homophobia. Because to be honest with you, I truly don't give a fuck how people choose to live their lives... Your lane is your lane. I'm slumpin' you because I just fucked-over yo' dude fo' alotta' bread, and you'a witness to the lick, That's it."

The trans' man looked at Ray Ray with bucked eyes before pleading.

"Please don't kill me. I don't wanna die. I gotta' get home to my husband. He needs me and I need him. Lord help me!"

Boh! Boh! Ray Ray casually planted two slugs in his forehead, then Smoke followed suit and strolled over to Ceelo and aimed the gun at the back of his head.

"Hold up Smoke man! Please don't do this man. I can get you more money, just let me live man, ple-" Boh! Boh!-

Crimson blood slowly leaked out the two holes that Smoke put in Ceelo's head, then Smoke ominously turned toward Ray Ray wearing a cold, blank expression.

They left the house with the money and jumped on a private jet two days later, headed to Detroit....

***

"Damn the city look different dawg," said Smoke as Ray Ray navigated the new Audi A-8 through the east Jefferson traffic.

"I only been gone two and a half years, and a bunch of shit done changed."

Ray Ray exhaled the Newport smoke before responding.

"Yeah, that's how it's goin' down these days dawg. Most cities always push toward makin' the home-front a tourist attraction, 'cause more tourists mean more money."

"I'm hip dawg. That's another reason why them silly ass politicians keep tryin' to build prisons in a lot of them lil hick ass towns. They be tryna' build up they lil weak ass economies at the expense of lockin' a nigga up, know what I'm sayin."

"Yup, I know exactly whatchu sayin. And speakin'

of modification, some things never change." Ray Ray pointed at the grey caprice that narcotic officers crept slowly down a side street in. Smoke smirked and shook his head negatively.

As they cruised through the downtown area, Smoke noticed a festival in progress. People were mingling amongst each other and being entertained by a variety of music in different segments of the overall event.

"Dawg pull over there, it's a gang of bitches over there just like it use to be." Ray Ray wasn't really up for it, but he did it on the strength of Smoke's eagerness.

After they parked, Smoke got out and let his eyes roam across all the scattered women. He paused when he got to the female wearing the low cut all white nikes with no socks, an ankle bracelet on her left ankle, tan knickerbocker that complimented her curvaceous body, and a white strapless belly shirt that clung comfortably to her hefty breasts. Her burgundy and black hair dropped and curved outward in five different layers 'til it reached her shoulders. And her mahogany skin-tone blended well with her snow-white teeth.

"Damn," said Smoke as he leaned in the car and grabbed his camera. He strolled over to her with his charm in full swing.

"Hey luvely, how you doin?"

"Fine," she answered dryly.

"Fine? Well you look like you doin' a little more than fine."

"Umph," she gestured nonchalantly.

"So what's yo' name sweetheart?"

"I don't think you need to know all that."

"Damn," said Smoke as he took a step backwards to look her over. "Why is that?"

She rolled her eyes snobbishly before answering.

"Because I truly don't know if you are worthy enough to even be conversating with me."

Smoke let out a slight smirk as he thought to himself, *"this chicken head bitch."*

"Well check this out baby. What do you consider is worthy enough to kick it with you?"

She placed her hand on her hip and sassed.

"Cute, warm eyes, and good conversation."

Smoke realized she was just teasing with him the whole time when he noticed a smile almost slip through her game face. He stepped closer to her.

"Is that right?" he asked humorously.

"Well that makes me overqualified for your acquaintance 'cause I'm so much more than cute, warm eyes, and good conversation."

She couldn't hold her smile back any longer as it spread across her face bright and wide.

After Smoke got Jemillia's phone number, he winked at Ray Ray as he produced a camera and stepped closer to her.

"Check this out Jemillia. Let me take a few snapshots of you so I can send them to one of my dawgs in prison."

At first Jemillia was hesitant to do it, but then she thought, *'what the hell. Why not.'* She began posing for the camera as Smoke snapped away. After the digital number on the camera read seven, he stopped and let her go on about her business.

He approached another cutie who wore a skin-tight Sean John body suit. The fabric of the hot pink suit laid neatly in the orifice of her muffin. Smoke drooled as it neatly outlined the shape of her swollen lips. Her plump ass absorbed the middle seam that ran down the center of it, which made it clear to see that she wasn't wearing any panties. His eyes traced her midnight black skin and stopped when he got to her stiff nipples.

"Damn, Damn, Damn," he said as he stepped closer.

"Hey ma, wha'ssup."

"Nothin, I'm just enjoying a few of the local rap groups. But I'm really waitin' on the Eastside Chedda' Boys."

"Oh yeah. You fuck wit' them huh?"

"Yup."

"Well check this out baby, let me take a few flicks of you for one of my niggas in the joint."

"One of yo' niggas in the joint?" she asked with a ill-looking frown.

"Yeah, one of my niggas in the joint."

Her frown was still visible as she blurted,

"Which system is he in, federal or state?"

"State, why?" Smoked asked curiously.

"Cause my baby-daddy is in the fed joint and he would have a damn fit if he saw some niggas passing pictures of me around."

"I feel you on that baby. But now you know you ain't gotta' worry about that, 'cause like I said, it's a state situation."

Her demeanor relaxed, and she unexpectedly turned around and peeked back at him over her shoulder. She slightly tilted forward, placed both hands on her knees, with her phat booty poked out and said,

"You want it like this?"

Smoke fumbled with the camera as she stood there lookin' like a model for the blacktail magazine. She certainly wasn't a stranger to the camera as she did pose after pose. And the one that took the cake was when she turned facing him, then grabbed her bodysuit by the upper thigh area with both hands and pulled it snug up in her crotch as deep as she could get it.

"Consider this the money shot and tell yo' boy to enjoy."

She mumbled seductively as she stood there knowin' she was about to make a convict real happy. Smoke snapped away and had to re-adjust his erection through the baggy sky-blue velour Roca Wear pants he wore. He slid the matching jacket off, and turned the all-white, with sky-blue trimmed Yankees hat to the back. His white airforce ones shuffled across the pavement as he made his way around her as if he was a professional photographer.

After he finished his session with her, he approached several more women and snapped several more photos. Some was taken with permission, some was taken without....

When the session was finally over, Smoke casually strolled back over to where Ray Ray stood.

"I had to take some flicks for my dawg E up in the state joint. He used to be my cellmate. Good nigga off the Westside. He gon' luv these."

Ray Ray and Smoke both suddenly wore bizarre expressions on their faces as Pooh's woman Rashia approached them with a bright smile. She was the last person they expected to run into. But they were happy they did. After the warm hugs and a serious thirty-minute conversation, they agreed to link back up soon, then Rashia left the festival with her new boyfriend.

The loud music that poured from the black Suburban with 24 inch spinnin' Sprewell's, grabbed Smoke and Ray Ray's attention.

A song from Young Jeezy throbbed through the system, and Ray Ray couldn't help but to think about how close his lyrics hit home. Especially when he spoke on things like, *"million dolla' dreams and federal nightmares. Then goes on to talk about being a real street nigga that wouldn't change for nothing."* It all just seemed as if it was a mirrored reflection in words. The only difference was the overwhelming desire that Ray Ray truly had in his heart to change. He wanted to be totally away from the street life years ago, but it seemed that he would always be trapped within the vice-like grip of the underworld.

And nomatter how much or how many good deeds he'd put forth, his bad deeds would always seem to outweigh them. And more times than not, he felt a vibe that told him, he would forever be Hood Driven.

"Humph."

He shrugged it off then focused on the short, stocky, bearded man who climbed from the driver's seat of the suburban and scanned the area.

Smoke noticed the chick in the hot-pink bodysuit from earlier, running up to the man as more flashy cars pulled up with sounds thumpin' from their systems... Suddenly it dawned on Smoke who they were. It was the rap group known as 'Tha Eastside Chedda Boys.'

Within a matter of minutes there was an entourage of about thirty of them... They stood in their group, drinkin, smokin, and socializing...

Five minutes later.

"Damn dawg, all eyes on us out this muhfucka." Said Smoke as members from the cheddar-boys shot mean-mugs in their direction.

Some of the younger members with lesser roles in the crew bobbed their heads to the music and kept their mugs on tight as they constantly stared at Ray Ray and Smoke.... Ray Ray started getting agitated and was about to address the situation, but Smoke backed him off and laughed as the youngsta's continued to bob their heads and lift their shirts to reveal the odds of the predicament.

"I see the homeboys still in tune with the D, ha ha." Smoke laughed.

"Come on dawg let's bounce."

As they cruised by them slowly, Smoke yelled out the window,

"It's all good baby, I'ma eastside chedda-boy too."

They slowly dropped their shirts and gave short head-nods as a gesture that the beef was ceased. Smoke nodded back as they blended into traffic.

"Dawg, stop by Strictly's record shop so I can cop they new shit and cop the Street Lordz new shit too. Them boys got some hot shit out here, foreal."

Ray Ray glanced over at Smoke with a curious expression.

"Man ain't them niggas beefin' with each other?"

Smoke smirked as he lit up a newport, then answered.

"Man, everybody beefin."

They cruised through the downtown area to do a little more sight-seeing, then proceeded to Woodward Avenue.

"Damn my nigg, these lil hookers done stepped they game up. Look at that bad bitch right there.... And look at that one dawg." Said Smoke sternly as he pointed at the light-skinned green-eyed hooker with the tight white coochie-cutter Dolce & Gabana shorts, a matching halter top, with white Timberland stilettos.

"Man Goddamn." Squawked Smoke as they continued to cruise by all the beautiful prostitutes.

"Ray Ray I remember when it was just broke-down crack-head hoes strollin' this terf. It must be some boss playa's behind the scenes on this trip, 'cause this a whole new ball game... Man fuck this, pull over," said Smoke eagerly when he spotted the dark-skinned 5'8 hooker that wore red leather pants that fit her like a second skin. She had silky shoulder-length hair, with measurements that made Smoke question her overall authenticity...

She strutted with grace in her red knee-high ostrich boots, with a short cut leather jacket that exposed her pierced bellybutton and most of her soft cleavage.

Smoke got out and approached her with a *'I wanna' fuck da' shit outta' you'* expression all over his demeanor.

"Damn baby is that all you?" he asked while pointing at her well-rounded ass.

"Yeah baby, it's all me. You like it?"

"As a matter of fact, I do. But what I like most is the fact that I don't gotta' run a bunch of corny-ass lines to you, because the understanding was established the second we locked eyes, which is,"

"No cash No ass," she finished the sentence for him.

"That's right baby, and bein' that I got the cash, you need to be gettin' yo ass in the car so I can put some more miles on that money-maker." She giggled a little before responding.

"Well since you put it like that, motivate me boo."

Smoke smiled and put five one-hundred-dollar bills in the palm of her manicured hand as she climbed in the car.

"Nigga you tryna' get us a solicitin' prostitution charge or what? You know them fine bitches like that be the police these days." Ray Ray questioned Smoke with skepticism.

"Naw dawg, I'm just tryna' get some ass. And I promise you bro, if this bitch is the police, I'ma still fuck her pretty-ass first, then kill'er. A'ight." The hooker gave a half-hearted smirk then re-assured Smoke that she's not the police as they pulled off in traffic.

****

After Ray Ray dropped Smoke and the hooker off at a hotel, he went straight to the safe house that he'd kept Sheila in the night he helped her escape. He couldn't take any chances on letting Smoke sex the hooker there because at this point, everybody was considered a potential threat to their situation. He poured himself a shot of Hennessey, spent some quiet-reflection time to ponder on the whole situation, then did inventory on all the weapons he had stashed there.......

Smoke watched intently as the fine prostitute worked the rubber on his dick inch by inch using her mouth only. She skillfully nudged the ring of the condom with her teeth and lips until the full length of it covered him... She strutted over to the television and turned it to the porno station. Smoke let out an audible "damn" as he watched her shapely ass bounce and wiggle with every step. She stood there with her hand on her hip wearing nothing but a red Gucci G-string, with a red camisole to match... She smirked a little as she watched the white woman ride the white man's dick.... After a few moments of close observation, she turned toward Smoke and stated,
"That ain't no ride baby. Let me show you a ride."
She pulled off the camisole letting her healthy tities swing free, then stepped out of the G-string and straddled Smoke's waist. Smoke guided her up, then down with both palms on each of her ass-cheeks. Her soft flesh protruded through the spaces in his fingers as he held on tight and guided himself upward into her wetness... Smoke rolled her over a few moments later, locking her legs over his shoulders as he dug deep into her

warmness....

"Ah, yes. That's what I'm talkin' 'bout baby. Fuck this pussy, make it cum. Oow shit!"

The sound of sex from the television coincided with theirs, and it only excited Smoke more to hear the moans and groans of two females instead of one. She gyrated her hips underneath him to demonstrate her experience in her profession... Smoke enjoyed her movement and became more stimulated as his penis bounced and twirled around inside her.

The session intensified and they both began to perspire as they moved wildly all over the bed... Smoke picked up the pace when he looked down at the beautiful hooker and realized how gorgeous she really was. He took long steady strokes and licked the side of her face as he administered the good sex to her.

"Sss, mmm. It's so good baby." She panted as Smoke slammed himself into her body, causing her breasts to bounce violently with every thrust. She suddenly wiggled herself from underneath Smoke, then laid on her side for him.

"Oh you want it like that now huh?" He waisted no time sliding inside her from behind. "Ungh!" She grunted as he went deep inside her from the back. He cuffed her soft flesh and toyed with her nipples as she worked her own clit and sporadically fondled his nut-sack.

Smoke enjoyed the way she pushed her ass back against him to meet his every stroke. It wasn't long before she found herself on top of Smoke again riding him wildly. And the way she moved the bottom half of her body had him mesmerized. It seemed as if her back never moved, yet her ass and hips gyrated as if they were boneless.

"Goddamn bitch, work this dick then."

She kept the palms of her hands flat on his chest as she worked her magic.

"Aw yes, gimee that big cock! Fuck my fuckhole you animal! Gimee your cock-juice now!"

Smoke almost burst out laughin' as he listened to the white woman on the television in the background. He suddenly noticed a slight change in the hooker's movement. She was a little stiffer and her nails began to claw into his chest.

"Aw hell naw," thought Smoke to himself.

"This bitch ain't 'bout to cum before me unless she respect the game."

He quickly got a firm grip on her waist and restricted her from further movement. She opened her eyes wider and asked,

"What's up baby, what's goin' on?"

"What's goin' on is you havin' too much fun, and that ain't what's up 'cause it's all about me right now."

She continued to try to move to keep the fast-building climax active.

"Come on baby not now. You know I'ma get you off, I got you baby. Whateva' you want, ju- just let me get this."

She started moving her hips again aggressively, then lifted her ass up along the full length of him. Then tried to quickly slide back down but was stopped by Smoke at the half-way mark.

"That pussy on fire right now, ain't it?"

"Uh huh."

"You wanna feel that hot cum gush out that pussy don't you?"

"Ssss, mm, yeah, please."

"Well, the bad news is, like I said before, it's all about me. But I'll tell you what." He paused for a moment as he allowed her trembling body to slide down another half inch on his pole.

"We can make it about you if you get yo' ass up and go put three of them bills back in my hand."

She thought about it for a few seconds, then jumped up and ran over to her stash and peeled through the bills. She made it back to him in a hurry and climbed back on top as she placed the three bills in his hand.

"My pimp would stump a mudhole in my ass if he could see me right now." She thought to herself as she lunged back into the session.

Smoke smiled discreetly before responding.

"That's what I'm talkin' 'bout baby. Respect the game and then comes the fame. It's yo' world, get yours."

The hooker didn't waste any time slangin' her loose booty in every direction on his hard flesh. He pushed upward to meet her every time she descended, which caused a smackin sound as their flesh collided, "uh, uh, uh, sss, oow."

Her breasts bounced fiercely as he stretched her hole and palmed her phat ass... Suddenly, she began to display the same characteristics as before. Her eyes hung low, she became stiffer in her movement, and she started to hump her hips more swiftly... She let out a sensuous whimper as Smoke brought her closer to heaven... "Oow, oow, sss,mm." Her greedy hole sucked him in as deep as she could get him as her mouth hung open and her eyes completely shut... Smoke continued to work his hips aggressively to give her what she badly wanted...

"Yeah, yeah, oh. I'm- I'm, oh fuck... oow shit baby!"

She dropped her head and Smoke pulled her closer to him and locked on her neck with his teeth as if he was a vampire. She moaned and let out a loud sigh of pleasure

as he sucked and drilled her pussy with authority...
Suddenly, he felt her body begin to rock and jerk violently
as the powerful orgasm sent wave after wave of pleasure
through her system... Smoke continued to suck her neck
and slightly choke her as he exploded shortly after her.
The hooker lazily pushed herself upward from his chest
as they both breathed heavily.

She rubbed her hand across his smooth dark face and
smiled.

"Now that's what I call unforgettable blackness,
handsome. And damn you bite so good," They both burst
out laughing as the session ended.

CHAPTER 11

As Ray Ray pulled up at the KFC drive-thru, Smoke sat on the passenger side of the gray Audi A-8 smokin' a Newport, bragging about his performance with the prostitute.

"I'm tellin you nigga, as good as I slang dick in them hoes, I coulda' been a pimp. I made the bitch gimee back more than half of the cheddar, and on top of that, the bitch begged me to be her new daddy. That comes from reading that old-school literature from the old-head playa's like Ice-Berg Slim'nem. They flat-out tell you how to break a bitch down with the dick and make her choose-up." Smoke quickly went into an impersonation of the character Goldie from the movie "The Mack."

"*Come on now pretty Tony, let's be real. Yo' bitch chose me. You know the rules. Now we can handle this like players. Or we can get into some gangsta shit.*" They exploded in laughter.

"Man if her pimp woulda' witnessed that, I probably woulda' had to kill that nigga."

Ray Ray smiled, then displayed a serious expression a few seconds later.

"Dawg, why you fuck with bitches like that anyway?"

Smoke didn't hesitate in his response.

"Cause bitches like that keep me on point."

"Whatchu mean keep you on point?"

"Like I said dawg, keep me on point. I'm a street nigga, and nine and a half times outta of ten, I'ma always be a street nigga. Most of them bitches that's out there like that is from the streets too. They just as hood as us. They probably had a bad break somewhere like us, and it came to the point where you either do what you gotta do, or let the cruelness of your society exploit you for all that you ain't worth. They hustla's Ray Ray. And the more I look at our life and predicament for what it really is, the more I respect hustla's in whateva' form they may come in. I can relate to their struggle, 'cause their struggle is my struggle."

Ray Ray gave a half-hearted smile before responding.

"A'ight dawg, I'll go for that. You answered that real eloquently. But what I'm talkin' about is yo' wifey situation." Smoke smirked then looked at Ray Ray with a silly expression.

"Dawg, I'm a man before I'm anything else. The bible said it best." *"The spirit is willing but the flesh is weak."* what can I say."

Ray Ray showed no expression or emotion, but in that respect, he understood where Smoke was coming from. With all the beautiful women in the world, it was truly difficult to be faithful to one. And even though Ray Ray's monogamous record with Sheila was only blemished once, he didn't completely fault himself because he felt that the situation that caused it, outweighed the mere act of sex. And all the times that he remained strong before then, he honestly didn't know whether to credit his actions to will-power, or his mental impairment that developed from the shock of seeing his family murdered as a child... Ray Ray paid for their food then pulled off. When they made it three blocks from the safe-house,

Smoke suddenly became alert.

"I'll be damned, Ray Ray, look."

When Ray Ray looked in the direction Smoke pointed to, he saw a youngsta in a blue kaki jumpsuit with a black doo-rag servin' a crackhead on the corner.

"Who is that?" asked Ray Ray.

"Dawg, that's dat lil nigga Packy that moved from Cleveland six years ago."

Ray Ray focused a little more.

"Oh yeah, it damn sho' is. I remember that lil nigga from back in the day."

Smoke exhaled the Newport smoke and shook his head negatively before he responded.

"Dawg, that's a shame that the lil nigga still curb-servin' tryna' get his weight up. Dat lil nigga probably ain't neva' gon' come up. I guess it just ain't meant for everybody."

They tapped the horn at him and kept going. They stopped at the speedy-photo development shop, then made it to the safe-house five minutes later...

After they ate the KFC and smoked a blunt, Ray Ray called and checked on Sheila... When she quickly put him on hold, he could hear the vacuum cleaner die, and a Kem song playing in the background.

"I think about the day I met, the perfect stranger, I think about us/ and I think about the day I got wrapped, around your fingers, I think about us."

"Okay I'm back baby. Whassup."

"Same ol same ol. I'm just callin' to check in on you and to let you know me and Smoke made it safely. You good?"

"Well, I guess as good as the situation gon' allow me to be. Have you heard anything?"

"In three days I'm 'spose to meet wit' them bitches, and

I'ma call you as soon as everything go down, a'ight."

"Yeah, alright."

"Where Ebony at?"

Sheila briefly paused.

"Ba- Ebony left a couple hours after yall left. And she ain't been back since."

"Well maybe she just stepped out for awhile."

"Yeah, maybe she did Ray Ray, but that's highly unlikely because she took most of her clothes with her."

Ray Ray immediately thought about how Smoke would react, so he decided he would wait for at least a couple days to tell him just in case she returned by then.

"Anyway, other than that is everything else alright?

"Yeah, Rob and Yvonne is doin' good. They still focused."

"That's whussup. Oh, check this out. Guess who I ran into downtown at the festival?

"Who baby?"

"Pooh's girl Rashia."

"Straight-up. That's cool baby, how she doin?"

"She still fucked-up about Pooh, but she good. She want me and Smoke to help her with a lil situation while we in town."

"Oh yeah, are you good with that?"

"Anything that got something to do with assisting Pooh, I'm good with."

"Okay, I hear you my love."

"A'ight then baby, I'ma holla back later. In the meantime, stay strong, and know that I love you more than anything."

Sheila didn't respond right away. She gently traced the mouthpiece of the phone with her fingertip while in deep thought, then softly whispered,

"I love you too baby. Please be careful." The phone went dead moments later.

****

"Aaaahhhh, sss, ahh shit Rashia... Damn." Marco sounded off as he convulsed and released a heavy load of semen inside Rashia's wet kitty. Rashia stayed fixated in the missionary position until his body relaxed, and he pulled his condom covered member out of her.

"I'll be back later, I got somethin' to do." He told her as he rushed out the door without a hug or a kiss as usual. But she didn't mind because she only viewed him as a means to an end.

Rashia truly didn't like him and despised having sex with him. She pulled out a photo of her beloved Pooh and kissed it, then whispered as if he was actually there in the room with her.

"Baby, that chump could never be you. And after I handle our business, I promise you, his bitch-ass will never touch your queen again." Then she momentarily drifted into thoughts of her real reason for dealing with him. Her slimy brother Buzz gave up Pooh's location to the feds and it ultimately was the 'cause of his demise. Buzz was released for the information he provided the feds shortly after Pooh's shootout with them. He then moved from the eastside of Detroit to Canton Michigan. Rashia was oblivious to his whereabouts, until the day she met Marco at an Ice-Cube concert at Chene Park in Detroit. She wasn't interested in him at first, but after hanging out with him a few times, she discovered the fact that his sister actually had a baby by her brother Buzz. She had sex with Marco the same day she found out. She felt that she needed to keep him in her space, because even though

Buzz was her brother, she vowed to make him pay for his betrayal against Pooh.

She already had Ray Ray and Smoke on board for whatever she wanted to do, because they loved Pooh too, and stressed that it would be their pleasure to help her punish a bonafide sucka.

The day had finally came when Ray Ray and Smoke were parked outside of the house that Buzz was inside of. After a twenty-minute wait, Buzz, Marco, Carlos, and Buzz's baby-mama all came out of the house and got inside the blue caprice. Carlos was the driver... It was around 7:30 in the evening and was fast approaching dusk-dark as Ray Ray followed the Caprice to a neighborhood liquor store... Ray Ray called Rashia before he made his move and asked her if she wanted him to kill everybody in the car, or just Buzz.

She replied

"Just Buzz." Then hung up... A few moments later, Ray Ray approached them all as they exited the store. He abruptly slapped Buzz up-side the head with the Ruger nine-millimeter, then let off four sporadic shots. Boh! boh! boh! boh! giving a leg-shot to Carlos, a leg-shot to Marco, a leg-shot to the female, and a shot to the front tire of the Caprice... They abducted Buzz, then quickly skidded away from the scene.

45 minutes later:

Ray Ray and Smoke both displayed satisfactory expressions as they stared at Buzz's restricted body sprawled out across the railroad tracks. They had each of his legs and arms tied to hundred-pound dumbbells as Buzz begged and pleaded for his life.

"Man we gon' Hoffa dis nigga." Smoke joked about the

situation.

"Matter-fact, the police gon' find Hoffa before they find this nigga." Smoke said things that wasn't necessarily true. He just wanted to instill more fear in Buzz as he awaited his fate.

'Whaaaamp! Whaaaam! Whaaamp! Whaaam!' The sound of the approaching train put the fear of God in Buzz as he listened to the loud horn.

Ray Ray called Rashia, then placed the phone to Buzz's ear.

"Buzz, I just want you to know, you truly took the only nigga I ever loved away from me. And for that, I pray that you die screamin' like the bitch-ass coward you are, you fuckin' federal rat! I'll see you when I get there muthafucka!"

"Shia! Shia don't do this to me Shia! Please sis, please!" Buzz yelled, screamed, and cried profusely as the fast-approaching train descended upon him...

The engineer didn't notice the object on the tracks until it was too late.

Buzz released one last,

"Aaaaaaaaaaaaaahhhhhhhhh!" as the tons of steel sliced through his flesh-n-bones like a hot knife through butter... When it was finally over, Smoke and Ray Ray left his remains on the tracks, then left without a trace.

Rashia was extremely grateful and expressed to Ray Ray and Smoke how they would forever be family.

She promised to never speak on the situation again and moved to Miami a few days later.

CHAPTER 12

"You see people, the wool has been pulled over our eyes for way too long. There's been too much pretending and not enough sincere effort by our government in resolving most of the issues that's become way pass problematic in our society. We pick up a newspaper or turn on the news today, and all we here about is how terrible and inhuman terrorist are.

And how our officials have just realized that their U.S. citizens have been committing acts of terror all along. Now they vow to approach the domesticated portion of terrorism as firmly and aggressively as they approach it on foreign soil, which is one of the key issues that I want to point out to you today.

Young people, I don't know exactly what my last statement sounded like as it came out my mouth, but hopefully it wasn't muffled, and it registered clearly in your minds. Because the message I just relayed to you is as serious as cancer and equivalent to genocide. Young people, your government has just professed a brand-new declaration of war against you. And it's coming at you through their judicial and legislative chamber, like always.

People, they've recently passed new laws that allows them to treat any gang member, suspected gang member, or gang affiliate the exact same way they'd treat a foreign terrorist. They've already began rounding up hundreds of gang members in various cities and detained them with no bonds and no official release dates. Some of the Hispanic gang members that's been living here in the U.S. from birth, are somehow getting deported to their native homelands, in which they know nothing about. And if you think that's bad, I can assure you, you ain't seen nothing yet.

So what I'm suggesting people, is that we approach these issues in a similar light as those who came before us. Our George Jackson's, Marcus Garvey's, Martin Luther King Jr's. and Ruby Dee's. Ruby Dee told us years ago that our mission should be to petition those in government to be more responsible, and more compassionate. Do things like, for example: get the prisoners off the stock market, then insist on the upgrading of the public school system for our children. We could also force those elected, to change priorities in government and the social and political arenas.

People, there are enough of us now to see how the constitution is being abused, particularly by Corporate America. So it's our responsibility to bring back sincere democracy and continue to strive toward making the country that was built off our blood, sweat and tears, respect our existence here. Because it's evident that we are here to stay... People, I'm no priest, but I do know lightness and darkness cannot harmonize. My mother's reverend use to say, *"Between truth and error there is an irrepressible conflict."*

"That's what we are dealing with today yall. But sometimes it takes more than the naked eye to see it. Luther's philosophy is referenced in Matthew 10:34 as saying, *"God does not conduct, but drives me forward. I am not master of my own actions. I would gladly live-in repose, but I am thrown into the midst of tumults and revolutions."*

Ya see what I mean people. It's no coincidence that I'm here today. I'm here because the positive forces of the world placed me here. Here to do one thing, and one thing only... Help resurrect my people. Now in the words of the rap group Dead Prez, let's get free yall!!"

The auditorium full of gang members, various ministers from different churches, and several representatives from the NAACP, all stood to their feet sending a wave of applauds throughout the room as Rob finished his lecture.

After the gathering was over, Rob casually approached Kay Loke.

"Man I wanna thank you for coming out like I asked you too. It means a lot to me because I know you are one of the few people who can make a difference out here in these streets."

Kay held up his hand as a gesture for Rob to pump the brakes on where he was going with his conversation.

"Whoa potna. You know I got the utmost respect for you, because you truly represented and held down our set when you was on board cuz. But you know I ain't no activist type nigga who can preach to the young homies about makin' peace with the enemy. If I was, I woulda' rolled out when you rolled out cuz. I came out here because you asked me too, not because I'm down with yo' vision." Kay paused for a moment before he continued.

"Cuz they killed Fatts a few weeks ago. And he was the only reason I might've even attempted to go another route. But when he left, that option left. And now it is what it is."

There was another pause.

"That was some good shit you was talkin' up there cuz, keep doin' yo' thang. It just might put us in a positive position someday. Holla back O.G Rob."

As Rob and Kay went their separate ways, the six pairs of eyes watched Kay eagerly from the red 64 Chevy Impala…. Kay-loke frowned when he was greeted by the two caucasion detectives as he approached his car.

"What now cuz, damn!" he barked at them.

"Aw, I think you know what we wanna speak with you about Kay. We simply wanna know who the car belonged to that your brother was murdered in. Because the female's name that it's registered to doesn't seem to exist."

"Well yall need to work a little harder on it 'cause I can't help you wit' that. I told you my brother got his own friends and I never even seen the damn car. Now if you gentlemen will excuse me." Kay jumped in his black 745 and pulled off…

The detectives pulled off seconds later following closely behind him.

"Damn!" yelled the driver of the impala as he watched the detectives tail Kay.

Rob made his way to Yvonne through the crowd, and they left arm in arm…

Fifteen minutes later, Rob pulled up at a gas station, and before he could exit the car, Yvonne gently grabbed him by the arm, stopping him in motion.

"Baby, I just want you to know that I am so proud of you. You looked so grand as you stood up there and delivered your powerful message. You were wonderful."

"What about handsome? Did I look handsome too?"

A bright smile formed across Yvonne's face as she

snickered.

"You know better than that baby. My king is always handsome. And even if he can't change the world, he should always be aware of the fact that he was the best man for the job... The best handsome man!" she quickly added as they both burst out laughing. Their lips locked and their tongue's caressed during the brief lustful kiss.

"Damn woman, now I can't wait to get home. You done got somethin' started. I'll be right back."

Yvonne watched intently as Rob entered the station. She patted her chest and let out a deep sigh as the reality of just how much she loved him dawned on her. She always felt that Rob came into her life right on time. And she couldn't imagine herself being without him...

As Rob stood in line to pay for the gas, the apple juice, and the beef jerky, Damon watched him from outside as he sat behind the wheel of the red 64 Chevy Impala with two members from his gang.

"Blood, why we follow this fool here?"

Damon casually shot an irritated expression to his friend before answering.

"Because we couldn't get Kay's hoe-ass 'cause one-time was all in his mix. So we gon' get that fool later and get this fool now 'cause he use to be they O.G before he went to the joint. Fuck'em. Now when he come out, yall niggas squeeze off 'til his ass ain't breathin' nomoe."

"Damon you only been outta' juvie D.T a good five days and ready to put in work already. That's why I fuck witchu blood."

They all shared a sinister laugh.

Rob casually emerged from the front door of the gas-station with a brown paper bag in hand...

Damon and the other two men fervidly stepped out the

car...

They walked toward each other without any detection of foul play...

Damon and his boys quickened their steps...

Rob still didn't notice them because his attention was focused on Yvonne. He didn't even notice when they pulled the red bandanas up over their faces.

They were approximately twenty feet away from Rob when a LAPD patrol car coincidentally pulled between them and stopped.

Rob stopped abruptly the moment he saw them, thinking to himself, *"Damn, here go these muthafuckas."* He stood there for a moment to see what they were gonna do, then shrugged it off when he realized they paid him no mind.

The officers were looking toward their laps at some paperwork with the interior light on. And they never even noticed him, or the three gang members with gripped weapons and covered faces.

Damon and his partners remained froze while they read Rob and the officer's demeanor...

They quickly realized the officers, nor Rob noticed them. And they wanted to turn around and go back to the car but didn't wanna make any sudden moves...

Just as the thought popped in their heads, Damon and Rob locked eyes...

Rob squinted for a brief second to get a better focus, and it was at that instant he knew his eyes wasn't deceiving him. He was an ex-gang member and was fully aware of the way the enemy came when it was time to put in work.

His first reaction was to strike out running full speed. But just as quickly, he scratched that decision as he stopped instantaneously in his tracks. He knew he was in a bad predicament, and it seemed like a no-win situation...

Then the second thought that he quickly entertained, came down to a matter of him putting his pride to the side and doing something that he was totally against. *Going to the cops for help.*

He didn't like police and could never imagine himself going to them for help. But he had to quickly remind himself that he wasn't a gang-member anymore. He was a tax-paying citizen who was making an effort to overcome the odds of a confused society. And if using the police as leverage would help him live to give another speech, he decided he would have to make that sacrifice.

He slowly approached the police car and began asking the officers for directions to a place that he knew would take them at least five minutes to explain the directions too.

Damon immediately understood his tactic, but he still stood there with his sight's locked on Rob. The other two gang members looked at Damon with demeanors's that said, *"Rob made a smart move, so let's get'em another day,"*

Damon was pissed because this was the second time tonight that the police fucked up his plans. And he was really pissed at the way Rob glanced over at him from time to time displaying a new level of confidence. Damon decided to ignore his partner's silent request and play street chess with Rob. It was his move, and he knew it had to be effective. He waited for a second until his eyes met with Rob's again, then casually looked over at Yvonne, then turned right back to Rob to make sure he read the play.

Rob didn't budge or change positions, he just continued

to play it the way he was playing it.

Damon suddenly looked at his partners, then calmly swayed his head, and the tightly gripped gun in his hand toward Yvonne. They immediately understood, then proceeded to walk in her direction.

"*Damn.*" mumbled Rob under his breath when he realized he was in check. His heart thumped frightfully and his thoughts stampede through his mind....

As they got closer to Yvonne, Rob came to the conclusion that he had no other choice but to totally abandon the G-code to save his woman's life, so without a second thought, he quickly alerted the officers to the gang members presence.

Damon knew that alerting the police was Rob's last move, and he wasn't sure if Rob's pride would allow him to do it until he heard the black officer in the driver's seat yell.

"Hey! You three!"

Yvonne never noticed any of the present danger as she casually rambled through her purse...

Pocka! Pocka! Pocka! Pocka! Pocka! Brrrrr! Brrrrr! Pocka! Boh! Boh! Boh! Boh! Boh! Brrrrr!.

"Check mate muthafucka's." squawked Damon, as Rob and the two officers laid lifeless where they stood.

Yvonne held her hand over her mouth to muffle her screams as she looked over at her man twisted on the pavement.

Damon slowly turned toward Yvonne. He stared at her for ten long seconds until his partners pulled up beside him in the car, yelling for him to get in... He winked and smiled under the red bandana, then jumped in the car and peeled-off with his homies. Yvonne was hysterical, and his dark face and cold eyes would forever be etched in her mind.

CHAPTER 13

Day 3….

"Damn these shit's is good man," said Smoke as he chewed on the corn beef sandwich that he'd just bitten into.

"You got me turned out on these muthafucka's Ray Ray." Ray Ray smirked at Smoke as he munched hard on his own.

After they finished eating, Ray Ray lit up a blunt of cush he'd rolled up prior to the meal, then turned the tv to the news channel. He hit the blunt a couple times, then passed it to Smoke.

And just as he made a joke about the possibility of him being on the news, a news flash popped up with him and Sheila's mugshots front and center.

The news lady spoke briefly about Sheila's escape, then everything after that sounded like, *murder, multiple homicide's, home-invasions, armed-robberies, extremely dangerous… G-Rider's!*

Smoke yelled at the tv as he laughed with the blunt in his hand.

"Dawg them bitches finally got our name right. They been callin' us Get Flat Boys for years."

"Man fuck that shit," Ray Ray snapped.

"We ain't called nothin. I told yall niggas a long time ago that we ain't namin' ourselves nothin. That shit is for muthfuckas that's lookin' to get famous off they crimes."

"Well Mr. sensitive, you know as well as I do that the authorities gon' put a name on you whether you like it or not. That's why I named us G-Rider's. 'Cause I figured like this, if they gon' call me somethin, at least let it be somethin' I wanna be called.

.... And speakin' of G-thang's, man you know after we kick out all this paper to get the babies back, we gotta lick a few muthafucka's to get back on top again. And don't get me wrong. I still got my Cali plug supplyin me swell, and my clientele is lovely. But I always did prefer gravy on my meat-n-potatoes, ya dig. So think about it dawg... Here." As Smoke passed Ray Ray the blunt, another news flash caught both of their attention.

"Thirty minutes ago, local police joined by ATF, DEA, and FBI agents raided the home of a young man by the name of Percy Smith a-k-a Packy, on the eastside of Detroit. Agents say the suspect was part of an ongoing investigation that led from Cleveland Ohio to Detroit, Michigan. Thirty-five kilos of eighty-five percent pure cocaine was confiscated, along with 1.5 million dollars in cash. The suspect lived alone and no-one else was arrested in the bust. More news at eleven."

"Daaaaaayumm!" shouted Smoke. "Dat lil slick muthafucka!- playin like he was on a low-budget grind and got dat work-work all along."

Ray Ray laughed as Smoke smashed his right fist into his left palm and steady bitched about not being able to peep the youngsta's game.

"Nigga if I woulda' knew he was gettin it like that, I woulda' got his ass a loooong time ago."

"Dawg you gotta' give the young nigga credit in his game, 'cause not only did he stay under their radar for a minute. He stayed under ours too."

"Yeah, Yeah," said Smoke grumpily as he received the blunt back from Ray Ray.

"Fuck it dawg, from now on I'm jackin bums-n-all nigga!"

They both exploded in laughter at Smoke's comment.

CHAPTER 14

Day 6… 8:25PM

'Bingo!" said Smoke excitedly as he hung up the phone.

"Man that was one of my Spanish associates from back in the day, his name Teko. He used to cop a hundred thangs at a time from me. He owed me a favor because I came through for him in crunch time a few years ago.

A major drought kicked in at a time when the feds had his money-route blocked, so he couldn't get nobody to let him hold the paper that he needed to cop until his situation got straightened out. Well, that's where I stepped in at. Not only did I not tax him like niggas do in drought time, I kept him heavily supplied with or without the money until he got straight.

Now he feels respectfully indebted to me for my graciousness. And the sweetest part of the entire situation is the fact that he know Deo.

He said they use to do business occasionally on that yola back in the day, and that Deo is one of them gungho type muthafucka's who think he da' shit. But peep game, not only do Teko got flicks of Deo, he got a location to go with it. So I'm bout' to float that way and grab that info. Then get ready to put down dat play."

"Okay my dawg, that's whussup." Ray Ray spoke jovially. Then Smoke continued.

"And the best thing about Teko's info, is if Deo hoe-ass

don't show-up at the spot with the babies like he 'spose too, at least now we'a know where to find his bitch-ass. And we can just go ape on that bitch like I'm dyin' to do anyway."

"Fasho. So let's go over this one more time. Deo says he wants to meet me at nine o'clock. So we can- *Riiiiiing! Riiiiiing!*

Ray Ray's ringing phone interrupted him in midsentence. He didn't recognize the number, but he answered it anyway.

"Hello." Ray Ray suddenly displayed a bizarre expression as he listened to the caller attentively for five to seven minutes before reluctantly mouthing

"Yeah, a'ight." *Click.* After hanging up, Smoke looked at Ray Ray curiously before speaking...

"Who was that, dawg?"

"Man, that was the man himself. Mr. Alverez."

"Is that right. So he the one that ya' old-man use to work for?"

"Yeah, that's him."

"Well what he want? Man his punk-ass ain't raise the ticket on the ransom, did he?"

"Nah dawg, nothin' like that. He talkin' 'bout he got a wift of the situation on what his younger brother Deo is on with me. And he wants me to meet him at the same parking lot I'm 'spose to meet Deo at tonight before Deo get there."

"You think he on some bullshit dawg?"

Ray Ray rubbed his chin in a curious gesture before responding.

"Even though shit is as thick as it is right now, and I'm not trustin' too much of anything right now, I gotta' say I detected a little integrity in his tone dawg. So Imma' go see where his head at, then we can stick to the script and get at Deo after I get my babies back. 'Cause you know I'm not lettin' this shit go. So go get that info from yo manz Teko, then suit-up and go lay on Deo spot until I let you know we got my babies back."

"Okay my dawg, I'm on it. And you know that as soon as I get a clean shot, I'm takin' it. I want this shit ended tonight."

They slapped five, then Ray Ray momentarily displayed an intense focus before mouthing his final thoughts.

"That's whussup my guy, but make sure you watch all angles, and do not react prematurely. I'll be atchu as soon as Deo leave."

****

As Ray Ray stood beside his car in the empty parking lot of a closed supermarket, he puffed on a newport and casually glanced around. He flicked the remaining half of the cigarette to the ground, then reached in the car and grabbed his blue-n-gray Nautica pull-over when he felt chill-bumps begin to form from the night breeze.

After checking his chrome 45 for the fourth time, he suddenly noticed an entourage of vehicle's slowly approach him. He squinted his eyes and used his left arm to block a portion of the irritating light as he stood there and watched them all form a complete circle around him, then come to a slow stop. The first door that opened was the driver's side of the snow-white Rolls Royce Phantom. A physically fit Spanish man dressed in casual attire stepped out and opened the back door...

A few moments later, the man known as Mr. Alverez emerged wearing a triple-white five-thousand-dollar Georgio Brutini suit, with matching Georgio Brutini shoes. He was 6'1 in height, which was unusual for people from a Mexican decent, with a full head of wavy hair that was a mixture of black and gray. His posture was a little unsturdy as he maintained his balance with a cane. His aged face contained small crater-like blotches and visible liver spots. He slowly approached Ray Ray in a humble manner, and once he reached him, he extended his hand and greeted him with a warm smile.

"Hello Ray Ray. It is a pleasure to finally meet the son of a man that I respect and admire in a way that I probably can't describe in words. Your father was an extraordinary man, and he earned his respect in his environment without compromising his manhood. And so far, I see two of his traits in you already. You have his firm handshake. And you most definitely have his eyes. Now, as for this unexpected approach against you, I want to apologize if it seems a bit untrustworthy. But being a man in a position such as mine, it was necessary to approach you this way."

Ray Ray didn't say a word as the man explained his disposition in a heavy latin accent. He just glanced at all of the henchmen that stood beside the vehicle's that had him encircled and gave a slight nod in agreement to Mr. Alverez's brief explanation.

"Now Ray Ray, I want you to listen carefully, because I'm not too fond of repeating myself in my old age."

Mr. Alverez gave a slight smile before continuing.

"Your troubles concerning your daughters demonstrate a great level of disrespect to my organization. My youngest brother Deo has always been a loose cannon... Yet he's nothing but a teddy bear. Sometimes I don't know what possessed him to interfere in me and your father's affairs, especially after all these years. I guess he saw a quick opportunity to make another small fortune on top of the fortune that he already has. But whatever the case may be, he was totally out of line. And as I reflect back on the latest events, I'm almost certain that he came up with this crazy notion when he overheard me and one of my colleague's discussing the anniversary of your father's five-hundred-thousand-dollar debt to me.

You know they say a eaves-dropper never hear things correctly. So he took the portion of the conversation that was beneficial to him and put his deceitful plans in motion. Ray Ray, the reason we were discussing your father's debt is because every year on the due date of his payment, we donate that exact amount to a drug rehabilitation center that we built and named in honor of him. It's called 'Ray of Light.' We did this because your father was a drug dealer that was truly against drugs in his heart. He would always express the desire for he and I to someday materialize a lucrative business and exit the drug game forever.

I admired his ambition to not only do it, but to invite me along on such a marvelous expedition. I actually gave it some serious thought, but I knew there was truly no exit for me. This lifestyle wasn't a free-will situation with me, it was inherited...

Anyhow, your father understood the game from a social and economic standpoint. And he never let his emotions supersede the things that had to be done when it came to being a successful drug dealer. And really, there's no such thing as a successful drug dealer, 'unless' you gain political power during the course, or immediately after your dealings in that arena. Now Ray Ray, I've heard many great things about you over the years. And from what I understand, you're a pretty gutsy guy, which is another trait you inherited from your father.

I know how you think and what you have in mind for my brother Deo, because if I was in your shoes, I'd think the same way and have the same things in mind as you. But I come here today and face you with the utmost respect as a man, to let you know that I can't allow you to harm one hair on his devious head. I can't allow it because in my family, it's traditional that we handle our own. So I'm asking you with all due respect, to stand down from whatever it is that you had in mind for him. And you have my word as a man, that I will handle him accordingly for his actions."

There was a long pause between Ray Ray and Mr. Alverez after his statement... Then Ray Ray slowly nodded a yes with his head.

"Ray Ray, I truly appreciate your co-operation in this matter, it truly means alot to me. And I don't want you to think I don't trust your word when I say what I'm about to say, but it's necessary for me to let you know the full extent of what you're dealing with. I have men on a 24-hour daily watch of Deo's every move until I decide to make my move. He doesn't even know that my men are watching him that closely, and he won't know until it's too late...

Now listen. I gave my men specific instructions to eliminate anyone or anything that tries to harm him. And believe me when I say this my friend, they are 99 percent accurate when it comes to the disposal business. Especially my long-time friend Pocco. So if you are entertaining the slightest thought of reneging on our agreement, please understand the penalty in its highest respect."

Ray Ray's nose flared as Mr. Alverez laid down the eloquent threat, but he maintained his cool because he understood and respected his game.

"Now here's what you can expect from Deo. He will always show up two hours after the agreed time. So being that he told you 9PM, he will show up at 11PM. And when he comes, give him the money, get your daughters, and leave. I'll handle the rest from there. Other than that, it's been a pleasure Ray Ray, and we will definitely be intouch."

Mr. Alverez gave a slight smile as he turned and walked back to the white phantom. Ray Ray climbed back in the silver Audi and pulled off. He checked his voicemail as he rode toward the safe house that him and Smoke occupied. He listened to Sheila's urgent message first.

"Ray Ray, I just got a call from the hospital sayin' Yvonne is there in shock because of something that happened with Rob. I don't know all the details, but I'm on my way to the hospital. I'll call you back when I know what's goin' on, love you."

The message bleeped off, then a message from Smoke popped on.

"Yo Ray Ray, check this out dawg, I got that info from Teko, now I'm sittin' a few yards away from Deo bitch-ass. I'm assuming you got the babies back 'cause it's way after nine. So if you don't hit me back in ten minutes sayin' otherwise, I'mma try my hand with this clown. Get at me."

Ray Ray's adrenaline shot through the roof after hearing both of the disturbing messages. Smoke wasn't sticking to the script, and was being premature in his decisions, just as Ray Ray told him not too... He had no idea that Mr. Alverez had his men on Deo. And any wrong moves could ruin the whole transaction.

Ray Ray frantically dialed Smoke's cell-phone number, but there was no answer. He quickly hung up and speed-dialed again. Still, there was no answer. He looked at his watch and hoped that Deo was already in route to make the transaction by the time that Smoke got there, but that was highly unlikely because it was only 9:45 P.M. And Mr. Alverez said that Deo was always late on purpose... Ray Ray quickly turned the car around and headed back to the drop spot......

Smoke sat patiently in the darkness and watched Deo and a few of his men as they made their way from the large yacht that sat on the riverfront. They walked toward the three parked cars and stood in a small group, casually socializing and smoking cigarettes...

Smoke looked over the photos of Deo one last time, then quietly slid out the car and made his way behind a thick utility pole. He began to grow anxious as he removed the large caliber weapon piece by piece from the duffle bag that he carried, then immediately began to assemble it without taking his eyes off Deo for long.

After gently twisting the last piece of the weapon in place, he meticulously pointed it in Deo's direction, and made minor shifts and adjustments until Deo's image appeared crystal-clear in the high-powered scope. Smoke revealed a sly grin, then crouched against the pole. He propped the butt of the rifle against his shoulder as he took aim. The weapon slowly swayed back-and-forth until Smoke was comfortable with the way the crosshairs landed on the target. Then with one eye closed and one eye open, he silently whispered

"Adios amigo." ...He suddenly looked down at his ringing phone right before he pulled the trigger, it was

Ray Ray.

"Whuddup doe my guy." Smoke whispered.

"Get the fuck up outta' there, now Smoke! The situation a little deeper than we first thought, I'll explain it later." Ray Ray spoke with urgency in his tone.

"But dawg, I got the drop on his ass." Smoke whispered again.

"I feel you dawg but fuck dat, bounce."

The phone went dead, and Smoke squawked

"Damn!" then prepared himself to leave. He raised the rifle back up once again to look at Deo through the scope before leaving... Struggling with the fact he had to abandon a open shot...

A split-second later, a silent shot rung out as the bullet exited through the silencer of the pistol.

The rifle dropped from Smoke's hand, and the immediate surge of adrenaline caused Smoke to dash off as fast as he could.

Blood gushed from the large hole in the side of his face, and his thoughts traveled at full speed as he ran fast and hard. He constantly cursed himself for allowing the silent gunman to creep up and get the drop on him. Smoke made it to his car seconds later, and just as he crunk up the ignition, Mr. Alverez's top gunman known as Pocco, leaned through his window with another silencer-tipped pistol and fired four rounds into his head, leaving him slumped across the console dead.

Deo, nor his men ever heard a sound. And five minutes later, two more of his men exited the yacht with Myonly and Love in tow. Deo gave a few hand signals, then they all poured into the group of luxury vehicles.

Ray Ray felt somewhat relieved about the situation because he felt that at-least he talked to Smoke before any dumb-shit jumped off. And everything was still a go.   A few moments after he concluded his thoughts, he noticed a silver –n- gray Maybach pull up with two black Escalade trucks in company.   Deo stepped out of the Maybach and slowly approached Ray Ray's car.   When Ray Ray stepped out, the first thing he noticed was Deo's highly distinguished eyes.   They were an unusual light cream-color, almost as if they belonged on a white tiger.   Deo was short and weighed about 165lbs with a receding hairline. He was in his late 30's and had a smile that made him look like he was always up to something.   The atmosphere felt eerie to Ray Ray. And they stared at each other blankly before one of them broke the silence.

"Where my babies at man?"

Deo gave a sarcastic smirk before responding.

"You'll find out as soon as you produce the cash."

Ray Ray reached on his back seat with a look of disgust eclipsing his face and pulled out four large duffle bags. He walked over to Deo and sat two of them in front of him while leaving the other two behind.

Deo signaled for one of his men to come over... Seconds later, a muscular Spanish man stepped out of one of the trucks with a portable scale with wheels on it.   He rolled the digital scale over to them, then sat one of the duffle bags on it.   A digital display of green numbers immediately appeared on the scale's small square screen. Deo nodded a yes to his associate then gestured for him to open the bag and get a visual of the money.

After that procedure was complete, they did the exact same thing with the other bag.   Deo knew exactly how much a certain amount of fifty's and hundred-dollar bills was supposed to weigh.   That's why he instructed Ray Ray to package the money in duffle bags in bills of 50's and

100's. Deo turned toward one of the trucks and gestured for the man to release one of the girls. A few moments later, Myonly stepped out and slowly walked towards Ray Ray. She ran and jumped into his arms as fast as her exhausted body aloud her too. Ray Ray held her tight, then briskly inspected her face and body for any signs of physical abuse. She cried profusely as he held her close.

"Daddy's here baby. Daddy got you now. I missed you so much." Ray Ray felt himself getting teary-eyed, but he remained under control until they concluded the other half of the deal and got Love safely in his arms as well. Deo looked at Ray Ray with a blank expression before he walked away and stated,

"I truly hope you understand that it was never personal Ray Ray. It was just business in the 21st century." He winked, then strolled back to his vehicle and crept off slowly as the two black trucks followed closely behind.

Ray Ray was overjoyed to be re-united with his daughters, but his constant thoughts of killing Deo wouldn't allow him to fully rejoice the moment. He questioned the girls once more to make sure they weren't sexually assaulted or anything of that nature, then pulled off from the secluded location headed toward their safe house. His cellphone rung five minutes after they were in route, and he swiftly answered it in hopes of it being Smoke. After anxiously saying "Hello!" his excitement faded when the recognized voice wasn't Smoke's. It was Mr. Alverez. And Ray Ray suddenly felt a bad vibe.

"Ray Ray." Mr. Alverez stated calmly. "I just called to say I'm deeply sorry about your friend. I take it that he acted alone in his decision to engage, so it won't be held against you. And I take it that you have your daughters back, so here's my suggestion to you. Rid your heart of any vengeance and live a productive life with your children. I was hoping you relayed the message to your comrades when I told you that Deo will be handled by me and me only. And I was also hoping that you heard me when I said to you, the stories that you hear about Deo are highly exaggerated, he's really a teddy bear.

So once again, let it go. Now as for your friend, you can locate his body at 2242 Chalmers on the eastside. I'm sorry it had to come to this. So, so long my friend." Click.

The phone went dead, and Ray Ray wanted to explode in anger when he learned of Smoke's death. A grisly expression formed on his face, and he fought with all his might to hold back his tears. He banged his balled-up fist against the steering wheel a couple times before realizing he was in the presence of his daughters, then irritably slumped back in his seat, staring straight ahead at no-one in particular. It was inside that he cried like an upset child as he attempted to conceal his true feelings from his babies.

Then moments later, he found himself shaking nervously as he accelerated into the darkness headed toward the address he'd just received from Mr. Alverez. He subconsciously drove beyond the speed limit and made it to the location in no time. He instructed Myonly and Love to stay in the car, then ran inside the house hoping to somehow wake up from the nightmare that was rapidly destroying his world...

When he stepped through the front door, he instantly froze in his tracks at the sight of Smoke's lifeless body crumpled on the floor... With open eyes, a broken neck, and a bullet riddled head resting idly in a small puddle of blood...

A few tears immediately descended down Ray Ray's

face as he painfully confirmed one of his best friend's brutal murder. He felt totally incohesive and desolate as he stood there. And he silently cursed himself for allowing things to become so complicated. A sudden image of his father appeared in his mind, and he felt that the level of trauma he was experiencing is what triggered the sudden reflection. Or maybe it was the fact that he truly needed answers from the one person in the world he respected the most, especially in times like this...

"Damn pop. Shit is all fucked up now. I' I'm tryin' to hold it together. But sometimes I don't know pop. I just don't know."

He mumbled to himself, then slowly bent down and gently closed the eyelids of his friend. And it was at that moment that his mind was made up. Thoughts of retribution flowed internally, and the decision to execute those who were responsible was officially declared irreversible.

Ray Ray had been down this road before and was all too familiar with what had to be done. It was etched in stone. And more times than not, only God could step in and save those who dangled at the end of his merciless intentions.

CHAPTER 15

As the group of federal agents filled the room, Special Agent E. Burns adjusted his wire-framed glasses and ran an unsteady hand through his blond hair before beginning the debriefing.

"Alright people listen up! We have another break in the Raynard Thompson case, and I'll be damned if I let this sonuvabitch get away this time. For those of you who know agent Barker, you should know that he's been working this case with me diligently since the very beginning. And he's made significant progress during each phase of this case. Therefore, I trust his judgement like I trust my own. Now, recently Agent Barker paid a visit to Raynard Thompson's deceased father's grave, who's known to us as big Ray. For those of you who are not familiar with big Ray's situation, I'll briefly fill you in... He was a big-time drug dealer who was shot and killed in a robbery alongside his common-law wife and a little boy whom the perpetrators mistaken for Ray Ray. Now, with the co-operation of the cemetery caretaker, Agent Barker made a helpful discovery. One that we feel is very advantageous in our efforts to apprehend this individual. Agent Burns stepped to the side and let the red-haired pale-faced Agent Barker finish the debriefing.

"During the course of this investigation, we've learned that Ray Ray was extremely close to his father. And some people say his father's death is what led him to his violent way of life in the first place. And after thoroughly questioning the caretaker, I learned that a black male has visited big Ray's gravesite and left flowers consistently once every three months for the last four years. And he's only missed one time within the four years.

The agent paused momentarily to let his statement sink in, then continued.

"I think you all know where I'm going with this, and if I was a gambling man, I'd put up the house, the car, and the dog on the fact that my gut is telling me this is our man. The caretaker informed me that everytime the individual comes to the gravesite, he makes a solid effort to be incognito, and he's very meticulous in his overall approach. So once we set up the operation to engage, I don't have to tell you'all not to fuck this up. He's not Houdini, okay. We'll get the bastard this time... So, if no-one has any questions, your dismissed."

****

"Unit one, this is command, are you in position?"

"This is unit one and that's a ten-four command."

"Unit two, three, and four, are you in position?"

"Ten-four all across the board command, and pop goes the weasel whenever you say so."

"Alright, hold your positions until I say otherwise."

As the several scattered agents concealed themselves in different locations throughout the graveyard, they watched the man that wore the grey-n-black Hugo-Boss hoodie approach big Ray's gravesite with three single-stemmed red roses in hand....

As the man stood there, he gently placed the roses on the tombstone, then pulled what appeared to be a pint of liquor from his hoodie pocket. He took a few deep swallows, then poured the rest on the surface of big Ray's grave....

The agents anxiously held their positions as they watched the suspect mumble a few words, then quietly trace the sign of the cross across his head and chest as he looked at the tombstone....

As he turned to walk away, a sudden surge of pain shot through his body as he elevated, then descended back to the earth in a violent fashion...

After being slammed to the ground with a variety of weapons shoved in his face, Agent Barker stepped forward and snatched the hood from his head.

"Who the fuck are you?" he asked angrily. -------- After a brief pause, the man answered.

"They call me Sporty, and what the fuck is this all about?"

"Fuck!" shouted agent Barker.

"Take this sonuvabitch to the station and interrogate his ass, I think he knows something."

When Agent Barker and Burns returned to the interrogation room, Sporty took a hard pull from the Kool cigarette, then continued to explain himself.

"Like I was sayin' gentlemen, big Ray was a good friend of mine. We go waaay back. He was a good man despite whateva' he did in his personal life. And I can vouch for that in more ways than one. I was flat-out down on my luck and had major issues when I met him. But he never criticized me about my choosing to be a low-life wino. He just continued to share words of encouragement with me and was always a lot more generous than others in his contributions to my sickness. In other words, instead of makin' a choice to eat a sandwich, 'cause I probably hadn't ate in days, or get a pint of Wild Irish Rose... With Big Ray I would eat that sandwich, and wash it down with that rose, ya dig. So why wouldn't I remember a man that was nothin' less than gratious to me and pay respect to his gravesite faithfully.

"Wait-a-minute" said Agent Barker curiously as he shook his finger toward Sporty with his mind in recollection mode.

"I remember you. You're the guy who owned the convenient store called Sporty's on McDougal and Theodore. You and your wife took a few slugs from some arab competition, and your wife died from her wounds, am I right?"

Sporty was instantly saddened by the frank reminder of the way he'd lost his wife. He never answered Agent Barker verbally. It was his beedie eyes and stone-faced expression that confirmed Agent Barker's words.

"It must've truly been hard losin' your broad like that. And actually, I remember viewing the crime-scene photos of her. There was a hole in her head the size of a walnut. It was awful."

Sporty was now fuming at the audaciousness of the piece of shit agent in front of him. He wanted to lash out at him, but he remained calm until they were through with their little bullshit game and finally released him.

3 days later...

"I love you and your sister so much, and I can't wait to see the both of you Love. Now put daddy back on the phone and we'll talk again later, okay sweetheart."

"Okay mommy." .... Love hesitated before passing Ray Ray the phone, then spoke into the receiver again.

"Mommy."

"Yeah baby."

"Promise me we won't ever be apart again when we finally get back together."

"Unhh." Sheila broke down from her baby's statement, but she quickly restrained her emotional outburst as she sniffed and wiped her running tears.

"I promise baby."

"Okay mommy, here's daddy."

"You alright baby?" asked Ray Ray when he got back on the phone.

"Yeah, I'm alright. I just miss yall so much and I can't wait for all of us to be together again."

"I know Sheila, we will be soon. How is Yvonne holdin' up on that Rob situation?"

"She is in terrible shape Ray. I've been comforting her as best as I can, but she is severely traumatized."

"Did you tell her about Smoke yet?"

"Baby if I tell her that, it would probably kill her."

"Well check this out Sheila, you just sit tight and I'ma hit you back later. I got a few more things to wrap up on this end, then me and the babies is comin' at you, a'ight."

"Okay baby. Be safe." ....click.

As Ray Ray headed back to the safe-house from the grocery store, he suddenly had a feeling that his mind was playing tricks on him when he spotted a man that was a mirrored image of his father's old friend Sporty... The man that Ray Ray focused on had Sporty's entire demeanor, from the way he shuffled his hands as he talked, to the way his frail brown body leaned and shifted.

Ray Ray mumbled to himself...

"I'm trippin, Sporty dead. They say everybody got a twin, I

guess that's his." He tried to bring closure to the situation, but in the back of his mind, he still felt that his eyes wasn't deceiving him.... The closer he got, the more it puzzled him... Suddenly, he pulled over to where the dude was at and stepped out the car while Myonly and Love munched on potatoe chips. He slowly approached the man as he stood there passing a bottle of wine with another scraggily-lookin man in company.

"Sporty, is that you?"

Sporty slowly turned around and briefly focused on Ray Ray before an excited smile began forming on his face.

"In the flesh baby-boy." Replied Sporty.

"What da' fuck!" shrieked Ray Ray as they gave each other a quick embrace.

"Damn Sporty, you comin' back from graves now? I thought you was dead old-timer."

"Well I thought I was dead too when them hot ones hit my ass. You know I had beef with them damn arabs 'cause my store had picked up and started crankin' harder than there's. Them pussies sent a muthafucka to do me in, and they shot me and my ole-lady up when we was closin' up one night."

Sporty paused for a moment as he thought about his deceased wife.

"Damn." He mumbled as the welled-up water in his eyes caused him to blink involuntarily.

"My angel died from her wounds man, an- and I lived from mine. But really, it shoulda' been vice-versa, you dig. I guess God didn't see it that way, huh? ... Anyway, man the feds immediately put a rumor out that I died too, because they was aware of the fact that I had beef with the arabs. And you know that wheneva' the feds feel that your enemies is strong enough to reach out and touch you, they automatically make the hospital staff tell anybody who calls and inquire about your status, that you're deceased. So that's basically why that rumor circulated like that."

"Damn Sporty, sorry to hear about ya' ole-lady. I know how much she meant to you man. But on another note, whatchu' been doin' for ya'self lately?"

"Baby-boy you see it." ..... Sporty opened his arms and took a step backwards to allow Ray Ray to look over his dingy attire. "I'm back to square one."

"Well check this out Sporty, I got some heavy issues of my own that's still in the air. And I definitely could use a thoroughbred like ya'self to help me bring clarity to some of'em, and closure to the rest."

"Yeah baby-boy I heard" Sporty interjected.

"So whassup Sporty, you ridin' or what?"

Sporty took another swig from the bottle of wine, then gave it to the man he shared it with.

"I'll see you around baby, be easy." He got in the car with Ray Ray and they headed for the safe-house.

Sporty explained the run-in he had with the feds to Ray Ray on the way....

****

2 days later....

"Now you look like the playa' you is Sporty." Ray Ray complimented Sporty as he stood in front of the full-sized mirror and checked out his taper haircut. With his brown slacks, gator shoes, and button-down shirt. Made by Mauri, and Hugo Boss.

The clothes fit his frail brown body well. And he felt like he was back in the mix again. Even when he smiled and revealed the two rotten teeth that sat front and center on the top row in his mouth. He acted as if they were pearly white....

After Ray Ray took Sporty shopping and gave him a little pocket-change, they went back to the safe-house to go over the plans that Ray Ray had in mind for retribution.

"Now check this out Sporty, I need you to be focused when we go on this mission, a'ight. 'Cause we can't afford to fuck this up. So, focused according to my definition means you bein' sober. So what we gon' do right now is have a drink to celebrate yo' sobriety in advance. And trust me Sporty, if we pull this off successfully, you can have all the drinks you want after that. Now peep game, we gon' be deep in the trenches on this one baby. And you gotta keep in mind that we dealin' with some serious muthafuckas, so I'ma stress it again dawg, ain't no room for fuck-ups. And the advantage that we gon' have on'em is the fact that they'a never expect lightning to strike twice in the same night, ya feel me? Now listen up." ....

After Ray Ray went over everything with Sporty, the only thing left to do was gather the necessary information to make it all possible.

You could always find a few men like Sporty in the hood. He could go anywhere in the world and blend in. The criminal world would be more doomed than it already is if Sporty ever chose to switch sides. Because the kind of information that would seem to take others a lifetime to get, he would get that same info in maybe a few days, or no less than a few weeks.

CHAPTER 16

"Myonly, Love, yall know that daddy ain't gon' never do nothin' to put yall in harms way, right."

"Yeah daddy, we know."

"Okay, good, because I need yall to work with me on this. Baby I'm puttin' yall in this hotel room because me and uncle Sporty got some very important business to handle. Now this is what I want yall to do if I'm not back in seventy-two hours. Go to the clerk's desk and tell her to call a cab. Then-," Love interrupted.

"Daddy you know I can call a cab by myself."

Ray Ray smirked at her spunkiness before he continued.

"I know baby, and I apologize for makin' a stupid suggestion like that, okay. Anyway, I want you to call a cab, and when the cab comes, take it to this address." He handed her a piece of paper and a cellphone. This is a private air service. Ask for a man name Mr. Ware. And he will get you on a private flight to your mother A.S.A.P okay."

"Daddy what's goin' on? I don't wanna be left alone, I'm scared." Said Myonly as tears fell from her eyes... Ray Ray sat her on his lap and gently wiped the saline fluid from her eyes with a hankerchief.

"Listen baby, I know you've been through a lot over the past few weeks, and God knows I don't want you goin' through nothin' else. But you gotta' trust and believe me when I say I will neva' eva' allow another person to do anything to harm you or your sister. Daddy feels that this is a wise move for all of us, and when it's all over, we goin' to Disneyland wit' mommy, okay baby." Myonly's expression became slightly less tense at the mention of Disneyland. She hugged him tight, and Love instantly joined in on the embrace.

Ray Ray had to regain his composure as he felt himself get emotionally choked up. He kissed the both of them, then re-assured them once more that everything would be alright.

"Don't use the phone unless it's absolutely necessary, okay. And here" .... he handed them both a can of mase.

"Do yall still know how to use this?"

"Yeah daddy." They both replied simultaneously.

"Well I'm sure yall won't need it, 'cause ain't no dogs allowed in the building." Ray Ray knew his joke was corny as he watched them both laugh, but whatever it took to put their minds at ease, he was willing to try... He hugged them again then headed for the door.

"Daddy." called Love before he reached the door.

"Yeah baby, what is it?"

"Daddy if you don't show up in the seventy-two hours that you plan too, what does it means happened to you?"

A half-hearted smile slowly formed on Ray Ray's face, then he answered.

"It means I'm runnin' a little late baby, that's all. Okay boo?"

"Okay daddy. Try not to be late." ......

Three days after Hurricane Katrina hit New Orleans, Sheila suddenly noticed a Hurricane Relief phone number and address appear on the television.: American

Red Cross Relief Center 1-800-Help-Now/ P.O. Box 94095 Baton Rouge LA. 70804-9095 …. After she quickly jotted down the information, she checked on Yvonne again, then scurried to the store and made a five-thousand-dollar purchase in the form of money orders.

She also purchased a *'Thinking of you'* card and sent it along with the money to the Relief Center. Sheila was the kind of person that would always be sincerely compassionate about disasters like that. She even sent money from her commissary account to the Tsunami victims while she was still in prison. Situations like that always made her want to switch seats with the current politicians of the world, because she always found herself pissed about the way they handled the relief part of natural disasters… Especially Hurricane Katrina.

****

As Ray Ray crouched low behind the neatly trimmed bushes, he pushed the button on the walkie-talkie and whispered into the receiver.

"Sporty, I'm in position, whassup with you?"

"I'm not quite where I wanna be baby-boy, but I'll holla back as soon as I'm in the necessary location, a'ight."

"Okay Sporty, be careful dawg." Ray Ray placed the walkie-talkie back in his pocket as he peered at Mr. Alverez through the Nikon Field binoculars.

Mr. Alverez laughed and mingled with several guest's as he worked his way through his crowded backyard…

As Ray Ray watched and analyzed the situation, he thought about how accurate Sporty's information was about the gathering Mr. Alverez was having at his home tonight. It was a private party, and the invitations were exclusive. But nevertheless, Sporty was Sporty. Ray Ray took advantage of the night because he knew it created a good atmosphere for the mission he was on. And so far, everything was in his favor... He was able to slip by security undetected, and secure a good spot on the large immaculate estate to watch from, until he got the opportunity to do what he came to do... Ray Ray hoped Sporty wouldn't slip up and let Deo get the upper hand on him. He wanted it to transpire as smoothly as it did when he'd first planned it. And if that was the case, Deo and Mr. Alverez would both expire on the same night at the same time, even though they were more than twenty blocks away from each other. Ray Ray tripped out on the size of Mr. Alverez's home. It looked as if it should be featured on MTV Cribs.

There were a number of beautiful women in company. Some laughed, danced, played in the pool, or just socialized casually as if they didn't want to alter their Hollywood appearance.

They stood there draped in the best jewels and expensive attire. They were adorned in Chanel, Prada, and Gucci-wear. Dresses by Marc Jacob blew softly in the wind, along with the subtle fragrance of John Varvatos for women heavily entertwined. There seemed to be an endless supply of various bottles of the most costly champagne money could buy. And the party went on inside, as well as outside of the house... Ray Ray suddenly answered the transmission on the walkie-talkie.

"Baby-boy, Deo is here, and I'm in position. I got a clear shot at this muthafucka and I'ma take it within' the next seven minutes."

"Hell yeah." Whispered Ray Ray.

"That's good news Sporty. And peep this, it's goin' down the same way on this end within that same time frame.

You know what to do as soon as it's done. And stay off the mic until you outta' the area, holla."

Ray Ray anxiously inched his way closer to the joyful crowd. And when he finally found a position he was comfortable with, he reached in his duffle bag and retrieved the unassembled parts of the 30 odd-six rifle... After quickly putting it together, Ray Ray eagerly found Mr. Alverez through the high-powered scope.... Sporty took another pull from the Newport then flicked more than half of it aside. The crosshairs from his weapon landed on Deo as he stood outside of his Yacht and chatted with a few of his henchmen. Sporty began to recite a silent count-down in his mind as he kept the weapon trained on Deo... Ray Ray gave a silent count-down in his mind as he kept his full concentration on the target... "Five" ...Sporty.

"Four" ...Ray Ray.

"Three" ...Sporty.

"Two" ...Ray Ray.

"One" ...Sporty...Bzzzz. Bzzzz ahhhhhhhgg! Bzzzz ahhhhgg!

Sporty screamed out in pain as the fifty-thousand-volt taser-gun punctured his body, and shot several waves of electricity through him... The cold steel that pressed firmly against Ray Ray's head, caused him to cease all movement. And the Spanish man that stood solid in his space, aggressively snatched the weapon from Ray Ray's hand. He ordered him to remain still as he kept the barrel of the 45 pressed against his skull and promised it would be lights out if Ray Ray tried anything stupid. The man casually pulled a cellphone from his pocket, and placed it to Ray Ray's ear... A few seconds later, Mr. Alverez's voice came through the receiver.

"Ray Ray. It seems that I just can't get through to you. You are truly a man on a mission. The wrong mission if I might add. But nevertheless, I've always respected and admired a man that would stop at nothing to get his point across. I've only met two men in my life that would truly stop at nothing, and I mean absolutely nothing. Are you number three Ray Ray?"

Ray Ray didn't answer, so Mr. Alverez continued.

"Okay Ray Ray, since I've always considered myself to be a fair man, I'm going to give you a better chance to answer my question. You should have your weapon back in your hand at this time, because I instructed my soldier to give it to you."

Ray Ray held the rifle loosely after his captor shoved it to him, with the gun still pressed against his head.

"Now Ray Ray, I want you to lift your weapon and look through your scope like you were doing five minutes ago."

Ray Ray's hesitation caused the goon to nudge the side of his head with the pistol and grimace

"Do it!" in spanish.

Ray Ray slowly lifted the weapon and peered through the scope... Mr. Alverez re-appeared in the lense just as he was before, only this time he smiled and waved at Ray Ray as he held two phones.

"Okay Ray Ray. I want you to show me you would stop at nothing to finish your mission. But, first let me explain something to you. Do you see this other phone in my hand?" He held up the other phone.

"Well this is a via satellite phone. And what I see right now is a very attractive lady on the screen. She has the sexiest almond colored skin, with the cutest silky black ponytail. And the red-n-black Victoria secret nightgown she's wearing is stunningly beautiful. She doesn't seem to be too happy in L.A. Maybe it's the fact that she's missing her two babies that were recently abducted. Hummph... Anyhow, take the shot Ray Ray, I'm right here." ....

Bzzzz "ahhhgg!" Sporty shitted on himself and blood oozed from his nose as Mr. Alverez's men continuously shot electricity through him with the taser-gun.

After Sporty finally passed out, they dragged his body to one of there vehicle's and tossed him in the trunk....

"Ray Ray, it's been two full minutes and you haven't taken the big shot yet. So I'm gonna assume that you do have limitations. I was almost certain that you were number three. Oh well, that's that. Now Ray Ray, you've disrespected me for the last time, and you've put me in a position where I'm forced to demonstrate my ability to run my organization without any premature compromises. The kind that some of my men may easily mistaken for weakness on my behalf. And, you know as well as I do that weakness among any leader, is a leader that's destined to fall. So whatever happens after this point, don't take it personal." After the short thump with the pistol on the back of Ray Ray's head, his limp body fell lazily to the ground.

Mr. Alverez focused back on the small screen on the phone, and watched as Pocco navigated through her home undetected... Sheila planted a soft kiss on Yvonne's forehead shortly after she cried herself to sleep. She slid out of the room and went to the kitchen... After downing the half of glass of orange juice, she made her way to the living room. She checked the doors to make sure everything was locked up and secure, then suddenly froze in her tracks when she noticed the curtain slightly moving from the night breeze that came through the open window... She slowly walked toward the window to close it, and just as she came within arms reach, she was startled by the intruder who stood directly behind her.

"Shshsh." He whispered as he stood there with the phone and the pistol aimed at her.

"What do you want?" asked Sheila in a trembling voice.

"Whatever the boss wants." Answered Pocco as he allowed Mr. Alverez to monitor the situation through the small screen as it unfolded.

"Pocco, complete the mission. Ray Ray needs to realize this is not a game when he wake's up from his nap."

Pocco didn't hesitate to slap a slug in the chamber of the silver Browning nine-millimeter. He took a step closer to Sheila and pointed the gun directly between her eyes. Sheila continued to tremble, and she contemplated running. But instead, she humbly dropped to her knees and leaned forward with her elbows tucked, her palms open three inches from her face, and her eyes closed in prayer... Suddenly, Pocco's grimacing expression changed. And he slowly lowered the gun.

Pocco was a muslim too. His mother was Puerto Rican, and his father was Arab. He instantly had a flashback of the three petty gunmen who walked in the Masjid unannounced when he was nine years old. They open fired relentlessly on most of the members that were kneeled in prayer... Five men and three women died that day, but fortunately, neither of his parents were there. Pocco thought about how that one act alone was more gangsta than most of the street activities he'd participated in throughout his entire life... And it wasn't even about drugs or money, just religion. Authorities later discovered that the attack derived from an ongoing dispute between members of the Masjid and members of a church only one block away... It was about who had the most clientele serving the opposite God.

"Pocco!" yelled Mr. Alverez.

"Finish the mission and come home."

Pocco didn't flinch or respond to Mr. Alverez's demand... Mr. Alverez sighed a heavy breath, then spoke again as he tried to suppress his anger.

"Pocco... Have you ever known me to be a man who seeks temporary redemption?"

"No Mr. Alverez," answered Pocco.

"So you are quite aware of the fact that there are no parachutes on this flight?"

"Yes Mr. Alverez, I'm quite aware of that... I'm also aware of the fact that the feeling of invincibility is okay sometimes, but only if you understand that anything that's truly invincible has never been seen by the human eye."

"Pocco, don't let your ego get you into something that your intelligence can't get you out of. Now do what I ordered you to do, or you might as well consider this the final chapter of your life. And you know if I write it...I'll write it in blood."

Pocco responded by pushing the off button on the phone, causing the small screen to go blank.

"Thank you brother," said Sheila as she remained on her knees.

"You're welcome sister." Voiced Pocco in a distraught tone.

Pocco stood there for a moment in silence, thinking about how diligent Mr. Alverez would be in his efforts to carry out his threats. Sheila watched his expression intently before interjecting.

"If you don't mind me asking, what is your name?"

"Pocco."

"Okay Pocco, my name is Sheila." There was a pause before Sheila continued.

"Pocco, I recognize that look on your face, because I use to wear that same one. Sometimes I would be so lost and confused that I wouldn't know what to do, what to say, or where to go to find answers. That is, until I embraced Islam. Because it was then that I stopped tellin' Allah how big my storm was... Instead, I started tellin' the storm how big Allah is. Would you like to make salaat with me Pocco?"…..

After Sheila and Pocco prayed together, he left as quietly as he'd came. And Sheila placed her small 380 caliber pistol that she held the whole time, back in her thigh-holster.

She'd managed to ease it out without being noticed when she bent down in prayer... She could've got the drop on Pocco and blew his brains out. But she spared him, on the strength that he spared her first.

After the prints from Smoke's body came back, one of the black detectives read the information sheet as he ate a hostess apple pie.

"Hey Jack, this muthafucka was wanted by the feds for a narcotics violation. He's been running from them for a few years now. His ass finally got what he deserved. Call the feds and let'em know that this chase is officially over." They both laughed as the other detective picked up the phone.

CHAPTER 17

Seventy-three hours later...

As Ray Ray slowly pushed himself in an upright position from the floor, he groggily touched the gash on the back of his head as the sharp pain shot through it.

"Bitch!" he hissed when he removed his fingers from the wound and realized he was still slightly bleeding... His vision was partially blurred as he glanced around the room. He blinked involuntarily a few times until his vision came in more clearer. He suddenly realized he was in an abandoned building as the foul odor, dirty floors, and demolished walls stuck out... Then a few moments later, when his senses were more intact, he suddenly felt something wet and sticky underneath him.

When he inspected closer, he saw that it was thick globs of blood. He quickly stood up and checked himself to see if it was coming from him... His pants and half of his shirt was soaked with it, but after his thorough body check, he realized it wasn't coming from him. He was instantly confused, and as he stood there searching his mind for answers, he suddenly noticed the yellow Crime-scene tape that had the entire room cordoned off.

"What the fuck." He mumbled to himself as he took small steps and glanced around... A brief moment later, the reality of the situation hit him like a ton of bricks. The house was the same one he'd found Smoke in, and it was

Smoke's blood that he'd been laying in. Ray Ray quickly began to make his way to the door, but suddenly stopped when he noticed the two figures laying in the corner of the same room. He slowly inched his way towards the two bulky figures, then suddenly froze when one of them appeared to be slightly moving... He strained his eyes to make out who or what they were, then slowly restarted his footsteps... As he got closer, the first image became clear for him to see. It was a Spanish-looking man in his mid-thirties, dead with two bullet holes in his head. He was wrapped in a prayer-rug with words carved in his face. Starting from the lower left side, up and around to the otherside. The words read: *Allah Couldn't Save Pocco;*

Ray Ray stared at him briefly, then focused on the other person. He immediately bent down and checked the pulse when he realized it was Sporty... He called Sporty's name and slowly sat him in an upright position when he began to respond. Sporty was still in bad shape from the damage that the taser-gun did to him, but he was able to talk.

"Damn Sporty, them bitches got the ups on you too?"

"Ye- Yeah baby-boy. They ra- rained on my parade."

"I see." Agreed Ray Ray as he watched Sporty sit there shivering with his arms folded as if he was freezing cold. His body released a violent twitch every eight to ten seconds, and a small trickle of blood oozed steadily from his nose.

"Sporty we gotta' get the hell up outta' here. We gotta' get to my babies if they still there, so work wit' me dawg. Try to stand up when I lift you." As Ray Ray got a firm grip on Sporty to lift him, he suddenly released one hand and clutched his nose from the immediate vapor of stench that came from Sporty's pants.

"Damn Sporty! They shocked the shit outta' you, literally huh?"

Sporty formed a half-ass smile as he walked out the house, leaning against Ray Ray for balance... Once they were outside, they walked about a block before flaggin' down a cab... After five minutes into the ride, Ray Ray smirked a little when he noticed the cabdriver turn his nose up and roll down the windows to release the stench that filled the car.

They arrived at the hotel ten minutes later. As Ray Ray and Sporty made their way through the front entrance, the first thing they noticed was a white middle-aged man running down the hallway screaming and yelling with his hands covering his eyes...

A white female staff-member rushed over to the man in an effort to find out what was wrong. Ray Ray quickly leaned Sporty against the wall when he realized the commotion was taking place around Myonly and Love's room. He swiftly ran to their room... The door was partially open so he barged in aggressively. Myonly and Love were standing in a corner of the room, hugging each other with fearful expressions on their faces.

"What da' fuck!.. Is yall alright baby? Did that muthafucka do something to yall?" ...Before they could answer any of Ray Ray's questions, he darted back out the door and charged at the man like a crazed lunatic.

...Four male staff-members managed to stop Ray Ray before he could make contact with the man... They quickly gave him a run-down of what happened and who the man was. All Ray Ray could do was laugh after listening to the mased man's story. The man was room-service.

When he delivered their food, he mistakenly left his

beard-guard on, and when Love stood in the chair and saw him through the peephole, it looked to her as if he was trying to conceal his identity with some sort of mask. So Myonly and Love opened the door and didn't hesitate to let the spray rip. They were yelling for the man to take off the mask as they sprayed him. Ray Ray understood that they were still a little shook up from the prior drama that they'd been through. And from that day forward, masked men would never set right with them again. Through all the chaos, the hotel staff never noticed Sporty, or Ray Ray's blood-stained clothes.

Ray Ray tried to camouflage the distress he was feeling as he phoned Sheila on the way to the safe house. He hoped she didn't get hurt because of his failed assassination attempt on Mr. Alverez. He could never forgive himself if she did... He couldn't believe the old bastard found Sheila so easily.

But after he tossed a few scenerio's around in his mind he concluded with the one that made the most sense... He'd tracked her down through Smoke's phone. A few moments later, Ray Ray's stress turned into relief when Sheila answered the phone.

They discussed all the shit that had taken place, and Sheila felt bad when Ray Ray informed her that Pocco had been killed. They hung up with plans to talk later as Ray Ray pulled up to his safe house.

As they walked on the porch, Ray Ray noticed a letter in the mailbox before they entered... He found it to be odd because nobody was supposed to have that address. He quickly focused on the return name and address. Eric Dorsey 617243 Ionia Correctional Facility. He briefly scoped the area, then walked in the house and opened the letter.

Smoke,

Whuddup my nigg, I got the flicks you shot me of all them cuties, and that was boss love homie. Ole girl wit' the pink body-suit on got niggas wantin' to trade a lil commissary for a little of her time wit'em in the shower. You know I had to get the shots of her laminated, she's my star hoe, (ha ha) And pimpin' still ain't easy, ya dig. Anyway, peep this, I need you to do me a favor. My baby's mama got a birthday comin' up in a couple days, so I need you to Scoop up a few long-stemmed roses and a red lingerie set... She comes through for a nigga in crunch time from time to time, so I figured I'd show my appreciation like that... she ain't ready for no Marc Jacobs yet, ya feel me? N-E-way, she wears about the same size as ole-girl in the pink. Oh, and grab a pair of Force One's for my lil man. He's two about to be three. The address is at the bottom of this letter. Good lookin my nigg... Until next time, stay sucka-free, the streets is watchin.

P.S. I come up for parole in 24 months.
Holla Ya dawg,
E.

Ray Ray fully understood after reading the letter, and he knew that Smoke must've really trusted dude to allow him to write to the safe spot. He tossed the letter on the table and made a mental note to handle that for dude later...

...3 days later.

After Ray Ray put Myonly and Love safely on a plane, he stopped at E's baby-mama house to drop off the merchandise.

"Sporty, run that stuff up to the door." Sporty got out the car and walked the bag up to the door. After seven minutes of knocking and ringing her doorbell, he came to the conclusion that no-one was home. He sat the bag inside her screen door and left...

...Two hours later, after Ray Ray and Sporty devoured a sixteen-ounce T-bone steak, they sat in the car and reflected on their current predicament.

"Damn Sporty, how in the fuck did we fuck that up. We was 'spose to slaughter them muthafuckas man."

"Yeah, I'm hip youngblood, but it's not that we fucked up, it's just that his game-plan was tighter than ours, ya dig? You gotta' realize the fact that his days in the game go all the way back to your father."

"Meaning." Retorted Ray Ray questioningly.

"Meaning, that while he was goin' through trial and error, hittin' and learnin how not to miss, you was just comin' up off yo' training wheels on yo' bicycle, ya dig. He paid somebody's cost to be somebody's boss. And in our case, he was just doin' what bosses do. He's a top-dawg enchilada eatin' muthafucka." Sporty laughed at his own comment, then quickly impersonated Mr. Alverez by talking in a heavy latin accent.

"*Ray Ray, I've already told you before, Deo's a teddy bear. Now stand down or else.*" They both burst out laughing.

Ray Ray shook his head and crunk up the car. And as he was bagging out of the parking space, he looked on the backseat and noticed a footlocker bag. He stopped and picked it up.

"Sporty, you forgot to drop lil man shoes off when we dropped that other shit off earlier." After Sporty released the bottle of MD 20/20 from his lips, he answered.

"I damn sho' did youngblood. Swing by there now and we'a drop it off to'em, it's only seven o'clock." Ray Ray adjusted the volume on the stereo and let the Frankie Beverly & Maze CD flow through the speakers.

"Ay youngblood, whatchu know about that. I thought yall gangsta's now-a-days only listen to rap."

"Well I'm a different kinda' gangsta. My old-heads put me up on them, and I been fuckin' wit'em ever since. And despite that bullshit European misconception about rap influencing a nigga to bust his gun, don't feed into it Sporty. 'Cause niggas like me will slump a muthafucka while I'm bumpin' a Keyshia Cole, Mary J, or Anita Baker CD. Don't get it twisted." They laughed as Ray Ray turned up the Frankie Beverly Joy and Pain and headed to their destination.

****

Sporty knocked again then took a pull from his Newport. He walked off the porch, then stepped to the side of the house and began takin' a piss. His body slightly twitched as his flow of urine came to a stop, and he briefly thought to himself, *'that goddamn taser-gun still got my old ass a little messed up.'* After he zipped his pants up, he suddenly caught a glimpse of movement through the window that he stood by. So he instinctively focused in closer... The see-thru curtains allowed him to see directly into the bedroom.

"Damn" he mumbled to himself when he noticed the thick, beautiful red bone ride a man's dick like a pro. He quickly waved his hands to get Ray Ray's attention. And when Ray Ray looked up, Sporty gestured for him to come over. As Ray Ray discreetly approached the window, Sporty spoke up excitedly...

"Look at that fine muthafucka represent on that pipe youngblood. Umph, Umph, Umph." After watching the performance for five minutes and noticing that she only had on the bustier portion of the red lingerie minus the panties, Ray Ray commented sarcastically.

"Look at that triflin' bitch Sporty. She got on the lingerie that her nigga in prison bought for her birthday, fuckin another nigga in it already." Sporty shook his head negatively as he cuffed his swipe and enjoyed the show... Ray Ray attempted to walk away but was quickly stopped by Sporty.

"Hold up youngblood, check it out. She switchin' positions." Ray Ray stopped and watched as the red-bone removed the rest of the lingerie, letting her nice C-cups swing free... Her swollen pink nipples protruded as she strutted around the bed... She rubbed her fingers through the dark complected man's low haircut, caressing his gray-n-black hair. Then she gently pushed him flat on the bed as she gripped his hard flesh and slid it into her mouth seductively.

"Lord have mercy" squawked Sporty as he watched her work. He turned towards Ray Ray excitedly to see if he would co-sign the situation, but the look he saw on Ray Ray's face killed his notion.

"What's wrong youngblood?" Ray Ray didn't answer, he remained transfixed on the woman as he moved closer to the window. Suddenly, his heart almost skipped a beat when he realized who the woman was... Then a split second later, his thoughts literally exploded in his mind when he caught another angle of the man receiving the oral sex. It was Syann and the snitchin'ass officer Smitty Branch who sold him out to the feds two years prior. He couldn't believe it was actually them.

He instantly darted around to the front door and began kickin' it with all his might... The door flung open after the fourth kick, and he ran up in the house in a raging fit. Syann and officer Branch were coming from the bedroom to see what was goin' on as Ray Ray entered the living room...

Fear blanketed both of their faces and their eyes bucked from shock when they saw Ray Ray. Officer Branch immediately tried to run back in the bedroom, but Ray Ray was too quick for his fourty-three-year-old sprint. As Ray Ray slammed him to the floor, he quickly grabbed the empty Moet bottle off the table after realizing he didn't have his gun with him. He didn't waste any time whacking officer Branch across the top of his head with the bottle.

He whacked, whacked, and whacked several times before the bottle finally broke. Officer Branch pleaded for Ray Ray to spare him as Ray Ray reached on the table again and retrieved a crystal ornament the shape of a nude woman and continued to whack him across his head.

The lumps that formed on his head almost seemed cartoon-like, and blood poured freely from the freshly made gashes. Syann constantly yelled for Ray Ray to stop, then she suddenly ran toward the bedroom when she realized it was no use.

Ray Ray quickly scanned the room for Sporty, and when he didn't see him, he took off in pursuit of her, leaving his barely conscious victim on the floor. Ray Ray caught up with her fast. He reached out and grabbed a handful of her thick, curly hair, yanking her back toward him. He slapped her hard across her face, then slammed her to the floor. She kicked and screamed as he man-handled her and started slapping her some more. Blood trickled from the cut that appeared on her bottom lip, and she continued to try to break free.

He put both hands around her neck and attempted to

choke the life from her. She violently gasped for air and clawed at his hands.

When she was almost passed out, he noticed officer Branch attempting to get up, so he released her and gave a swift kick to officer Branch's mouth. Then ran in the bedroom and snatched the Polo sheet from her bed.

He went straight to the kitchen from the bedroom and fumbled around for a few seconds, then returned with the sheet, a knife, and a small container of lighter fluid. He put a slit in the sheet with the knife, then tore a long strip from it. He rolled officer Branch over and tied his hands behind his back. Then tore off another strip and tied Syann up. He stood up over them breathing heavy with the expression of a crazed man.

"Whuddup officer Snitch! Nigga I thought we had a understanding wit' each other. I thought you was one of those niggas who respected the game when it came to the street-life. Especially when a nigga paid you as swell as I did. But naw naw, you go and send the feds to Amsterdam to disturb me and my family's beautiful life. And caused all kinds of bullshit to jump off for us. Man you actually looked happy when we killed that federal agent, and then you betray me. But it's all good, 'cause I'ma fix you up real good. It's only right that I show my appreciation."

Officer Branch pleaded for his life as Ray Ray casually doused his head and face with the lighter fluid. He pulled a lighter from his pocket and turned towards Syann.

"Make sho' you pay close attention bitch, 'cause you next."

Ray Ray flicked the lighter and placed it under officer Branch's chin. The flames immediately became engulfed over his entire head. He screamed and wiggled on the floor wildly as his skin sweltered and bubbled from the hot blaze. Syann began to scream as she watched the situation unfold.

Ray Ray turned toward her and demanded her to shut the fuck up, then instantly began dousing her head and face with the accelerant. She rolled her head around and tried to dodge the flammable liquid as it ran from her head down into her bossom.

As Ray Ray focused his attention on her, officer Branch suddenly sprung up from the floor. The flames had burned his tied hands a loose, and when Ray Ray turned around, he noticed officer Branch running full speed toward the door... He also noticed Sporty coming through the front door at that very instant with a tire-iron in hand.

"Sporty! Get that muthafucka!" Ray Ray shouted anxiously, and Sporty responded by swinging the tire-iron with all his might. Crack! The cold steel caught officer Branch on his left shoulder, but due to the speed he'd built up, it wasn't enough to stop him. He blew right pass Sporty with his head still engulfed in flames and made it to his car. And by the time Ray Ray made it to the front door, he was greeted by the screeching tires on the beige Cadallac Deville.

"Damn!" mumbled Ray Ray as he watched him float up the street swirvin' and side-swiping parked cars until he bent a corner and was out of sight. Ray Ray emphatically rejoined Syann as she continued to try to break free. He slapped her again, then pulled the lighter from his pocket. He flicked it a couple times but was unsuccessful in his attempt to infuse a flame.

As he continued to flick it, Syann frantically yelled,

"No Ray Ray, Please! not in front of your son!" ...Ray Ray paused for a moment, then delivered a hard slap across her face.

"Aagh!" she screamed out as her stinging face turned cherry red. But despite the pain, she yelled out again.

"I know you hate me and wanna kill me, but please don't do it in front of your son!"

Ray Ray ignored her plea's and finally sparked a tall flame on the lighter. He leaned toward her face as she cringed and back-pedaled away... And just as he was about to make contact, Sporty spoke up.

"Ray Ray, hold up youngblood! Hold up!" Ray Ray paused for a moment, then looked back to see what was up. Sporty casually pointed at her two-year-old son that was standing in the room with a low, steady cry with tears streaming down his brown face. As Ray Ray looked at the little man, Syann anxiously used the moment to do some necessary explaining.

"Ray Ray, that night we had sex, I-I put a hole in the condom. And I prayed to God that I would get pregnant. Ray Ray you know how I feel about you. And having your baby meant the world to me. Ray Ray I lov-"
"Bitch shut the fuck up! Just shut up!" Ray Ray snapped at her as he eagerly held the trained lighter only inches from her face.

He wanted to dispute her accusations and tell her she was a no-good low-down dirty connivan bitch. A fake, a phony, a flat out lier, then set her body ablaze, but the appearance of the little man who stood there in front of him, made it all irrelevant. He was a spitting image of Ray Ray. His resemblance to Ray Ray was so close, that it seemed as if Ray Ray had personally given birth to him. Sporty stood there shaking his head negatively as he marveled over the resemblance of Ray Ray and the child....

Suddenly, Ray Ray slammed the lighter into the wall, then delivered another vicious slap to her already bruised face.

"You scandalous bitch! Bitch I should still kill yo' ass."

He snatched her to her feet and aggressively shoved her into her bedroom. As she sat on the bed with her head hung low, he immediately began his interrogation.

"Bitch, at first I kept askin' myself, why would this dizzy hoe tell me she gon' help me get my wife outta prison, accept my ten G's, make me give her some dick, then play me. Knowin' damn well I'm on some G-shit. But after I gave the whole situation some serious thought, I finally concluded that you just a crazy bitch. You the kind'a bitch that get off on playin' wit fire. And it's just a matter of time befoe' yo' silly ass get burned, literally."

"Look who's talkin," Syann silently thought to herself before responding.

"Ray Ray I didn't mean to hurt you, I knew how much you loved Sheila, and mentioning her name was the only way I could get what I wanted from you. But aside from that, I've never crossed you Ray Ray. Think back for a minute. I could've easily set you up for niggas to get you, because a few top dawgs came at me askin' me have I ever accommodated you in my private call-girl service. I told them no, despite the money they offered." She put strong emphasis on the last part of her statement, then continued.

"And everytime any law enforcement person asked me questions about you, I told them I didn't know nothin' about you Ray Ray. The bottom line is, I love you."

"Well start lovin' a muthafucka that's gon' love you back," Ray Ray snapped, then began pacing the floor in front of her... After a few moments of silence, he stopped in front of her again.

"Now tell me this, how in the fuck did you hook up with officer Branch?"

"Ray Ray, he is just one of the muthafuckas that I trick with from time to time. He pay good."

"Do you know where he live at?"

"Naw, because he knows I use to be connected with you, and he didn't trust letting me know where he lives. He is scared to death of you, and all he use to talk about is how he hope the feds hurry up and catch you so you wouldn't ever show up in Detroit again. He ain't a cop nomore, but the feds is workin' on somethin' with him that might get him reinstated. I think it got somethin' to do with some more snitchin.'"

Ray Ray paused for a moment and let her words sink in before responding.

"Well check this out, is it any way you can get in touch with him?"

"Yeah, but it's gon' be hella' difficult after what just happened. Because he probably think I set him up, and he gon' be leery as hell for awhile."

"Well start workin' on it A.S.A.P and find out what hospital he went to, a'ight?"

"Alright." Syann agreed. And despite all that was goin' on, she couldn't help but feel joyful about Ray Ray needing her again. Blood instantly rushed to her loins as she sat there with her wounded arm cradled. And the moisture between her legs caused her to squeeze her knees together tightly.

"Ray Ray, do you want a blood test for our son?"

"You damn right I want a blood test. And let me ask you this. (If) he mine, why you got dude up in the joint thinkin' it's his?"

174

"Because E is a good dude, and he was there for me through some rough times."

"Rough times huh?"

"Yeah, rough times Ray Ray. Plus, I ain't know if I was gon' ever see you again."

"So how you think he gon' feel if you tell'em the baby ain't his?"

"I'm quite sure he's gonna feel disrespected, but he'a get over it. Oh, and by the way, your son's name is Raynard Jr. a-k-a lil Ray."

Ray Ray thought to himself,

"This bitch is still a king-cobra. Some things never change."
He instructed her to pack a few things because they all would stay in a motel overnight. He didn't wanna chance staying at her house after what had just happened. And he didn't wanna allow her to see the safe house just yet.

CHAPTER 18

Ray Ray gripped the gun in his waist discreetly as he sat in the waiting room of the small doctor's office. He stopped by the safe house the night before and picked up a weapon for himself, and a weapon for Sporty so he could sleep better around Syann.

After the 45-minute wait, Syann's middle-aged African American doctor appeared in the doorway of his office, then signaled for them to come inside. He briefly explained the procedure, then sterilized his hands and ran a cotton Q-tipped swab in the corner of her son's mouth.

When he was done with him, he did the same thing to Ray Ray. The doctor gave Ray Ray the option to pay for speedy results or wait the standard two weeks to find out. Ray Ray paid cash for the speedy service, then waited for an hour for the outcome. While he waited, he thought about the negative effect that the issue would have on Sheila. He knew she was a devout wife and a loyal friend. But situations like this could reveal a side of a woman that would put true love in harms way. And could possibly destroy everything they ever stood for as a couple. Ray Ray was aware of the fact that there was no such thing as a perfect woman, but he was convinced in his heart and mind that she was the closest he'd ever get to it.

His thoughts constantly raced as he sat there and entertained the possibility of a worse-case scenario. He wished he could keep it from her, but he knew he could never do that. Nor could he ever walk away from a child that belonged to him. Ray Ray always wanted a son, but he wanted all of his children to come into the world through Sheila's womb. He'd planned it that way since the day he confessed his love to her. But sometimes, all plans don't go as planned.

"99.99 percent positive," said the Doctor as he read from the paper that was fresh out of the fax machine. His words seemed to be in slow motion as they penetrated Ray Ray's eardrums, while Syann displayed an expression of pure satisfaction.

"Are you sure about that doc?" asked Ray Ray in a disappointing tone.

"Yes sir, I'm sure. DNA don't make mistakes."

Ray Ray slightly dropped his head, then stood up a few seconds later and approached the two-year-old man-child.

"Well lil man, it is what it is. Let's go." He casually took him by the hand and strolled out of the doctor's office, while Syann and Sporty followed closely behind.

CHAPTER 19

"What do you mean your trip is gon' be delayed Ray Ray?" Sheila paced the floor peevishly as she spoke to Ray Ray over the phone.

"Baby something heavy came up, and I need you to just stay put until I get there."

"No Ray Ray, I need to see you. I'm gettin' on a plane and I'll be there late tomorrow. Because I'm really not liking the sound of your voice, so be expecting me."

"Sheila what about the babies?" Ray Ray tried to find any logical excuse to make her stay where she was.

"Yvonne will watch'em."

"Sheila I thought you said Yvonne was a little unsteady right now."

"She is, but she's doin' much better and she's steady enough to watch them. I'll talk to you later and let you know what time I'll make it to Detroit."

"No Sheila!- what part of no don't you understand? I'm tryna' tell you that it's too much bullshit jumpin' off right now. It's way too hot up here for you to risk bein' seen by some patriotic muthafucka tryna' to do his city a good deed. They been showin' yo' face on every news channel every hour. So stay where you at 'til I get there."

"Well tell me what the hell is wrong Ray Ray. What all of a sudden came up?"

"Sheila, I gotta make a few moves to put us back in a

financial comfort zone, a'ight."

"Ray Ray are you serious?" Sheila asked in a tone of disbelief.

"You damn right I'm serious. What da' fuck I'm 'spose to do, let my family starve?"

"Ray Ray it's not that serious, we will get by."

"What the hell you mean it's not that serious. That's a helluva statement from a person in your shoes. You been drinkin' or something. Huh?"

Sheila released a skittish smirk, then sighed.

"You know what Ray Ray, this is not about us. It never has been. This is about you Ray Ray."

"And what's that 'spose to mean Sheila?"

"It means that you actually think you're in your natural element when you do the wicked shit you do. You seem to always find and excuse to put ya'self right back in the mix of chaos and havoc. Ain't you tired of dodgin' death and takin' penitentiary chances man? You seem to look forward to it Ray Ray." Sheila's voice began to crackle as she remained reluctant to back down from getting her point across.

"Ray Ray you're in love with the chase. And I sometimes wonder, will the man that I love ever catch up to what it is he's really chasin."

"Sheila now you soundin' like a damn criminologist-n-shit. I don't know what prison did to you, but whenever you stop bein' in denial and really look at that reflection in your mirror, maybe you'a see that we shoulda' had the same DNA. 'Cause we identical in character. Just think about it, when I feel that something is wrong, I try my damnest to make it right. And when you feel something is wrong, you try your damnest to make it right. We been standin' firm on the shit that we perceive to be right from day one, nomatter who didn't agree with us, we still did us. And it ain't no doubt in my mind that you wouldna' came through for me exactly like I came through for you if I was in prison, Or you woulda' died tryin... am I right?"

"Yes Ray Ray, you're right... But now that our predicament is so sensitive, we can't keep adding fuel to the fire, we gotta think baby. Allah says-"

"Hold up Shei, don't go there wit' me. You know I don't get down like that."

"Get down like what Ray Ray?" Sheila became more defensive. Not trying to hide the irritation in her voice.

"Get down with that religious persuasion. And don't get me wrong baby, I respect your stance in what you believe in. But you know I don't operate like that. I don't base my life off none of those doctored-up belief systems. My belief comes from within. Meaning, that whenever I find myself in a jam, I resort to my knowledge of the streets to remove me from that jam. Oppose to standin' still prayin to God, hopin that he magically teleports me up outta' the situation, know what I mean."

"Naw, I don't know what you mean. And answer me this. Who do you think is responsible for keepin' you outta' harms way all this time?"

"Do you really want me to answer that after all that I just told you?"

"Yes I do, so don't hold me up." Sheila sassed.

"Okay, I'll tell you who I think is responsible... Me and my ability to slump a muthafucka without hesitation. Along with my ability to approach the streets on the level the streets call for."

Sheila paused for a moment, and Ray Ray could tell that he'd struck a nerve, so he quickly came back at her with a more subtle approach.

"Listen baby, I understand where you comin' from, but this shit is similar to bein' on a basketball court. When I'm out there, I gotta play the game to win… And winning means I gotta' try to block every shot, get every rebound, every assist, and try to make every shot count. Then come home and feed my family. Know what I'm sayin Shei?"

Sheila's voice was beginning to sound low and worn.

"Ray Ray, most of the time people walk away from basketball games, win, lose, or draw. But that's not always the case with street games."

Ray Ray was tired of the debate, because he knew there was no way she would ever agree with his being wrapped up in a game that could 'cause him to possibly be killed in the blink of an eye, so he decided to set a different tone to the conversation to somewhat brace her for what he wanted to tell her next.

"Yeah, that might be true baby, but not if I got my superwoman on my side. She's faster than that white-boy Billy the kid. And slicker than a oil-spill on Bush-highway, you ain't heard."

Sheila released a little giggle, and Ray Ray felt a little more at ease since he had her smiling.

"Sheila, check this out baby." He spoke seriously.

"Do you realize that you are the ground that I walk on, and the oxygen that I breathe?"

"Yes Ray Ray."

"And do you understand that when took our wedding vows, it meant 'til death do us part, literally. And that I would never hold nothin' back from you?"

"Yes."

Ray Ray glanced at the almost three-year-old toddler for a moment as he slept peacefully in one of the hotel beds, then focused back to Sheila.

"Well, I didn't wanna' do this over the phone, but it's somethin' that I need to holla atchu about. And ain't no sense in procrastinating, so listen up."

After Ray Ray had finished running the whole Syann situation down to Sheila, and explained how his illegitimate child had came about, the only response he heard was the uncontrollable sniffle's from Sheila's constant crying... Then moments later, the phone went dead. Ray Ray tried to call back twenty times in a row, letting the phone ring twelve and thirteen times a call. And each time that he was forced to hang up without an answer, his heart felt a thousand pounds heavier.

Syann had eaves-dropped on most of the conversation, then slid in the bathroom when she became disgusted at how many times Ray Ray professed his love for Sheila. She fidgeting removed the small bag of white powder from her purse, then dipped her manicured pinky-nail in and scooped up a small portion. The powder evaporated gracefully as she placed it at the opening of her left nostril. Then the second scoop vanished just as easily only seconds later.... She tilted her head back for a moment to allow the cocaine to propel deeper into her system, then sat there on the toilet with a glare in her eyes and reflected on her complicated life.

As Ray Ray paced the floor back and forth, fervently bothered about the situation with Sheila, Sporty casually approached him.

"Whassup youngblood. You gon' be a'ight?"

Ray Ray was hesitant in his response because Sporty's words made a late registration through his swarm of thoughts.

"I really don't know Sporty. 'Cause Sheila takin' this shit

hard man."

"Well, we anticipated that youngblood. But in critical times like these, it's important to remain focused, you dig. Now pull ya'self together baby and tell me what's next for us." Ray Ray stared blankly for a few seconds, then began to nod in agreement with Sporty.

"Yeah Sporty, I feel you man. And what's next for us is more currency. Know what I'm sayin."

"I'm wit' it man. Who you got in mind?"

"Man, that bitch in the bathroom told me about a few heavyweights she be servin' up from time to time, so that's who I got in mind so far."

Sporty took a full minute to respond. He scratched the right side of his head, then focused intently on Ray Ray.

"Youngblood, that just might be all good, but I'ma be straight-up witchu family, I truly don't trust that broad. So keep a real close watch on that beautiful muthafucka, 'cause I'll be damned if we let her get us fucked up, you dig."

"Yeah, I hear ya Sporty. And please believe if that bitch so-much-as sneeze wrong around us, we'a be goin' bowlin with her head and usin' the rest of her ass for swamp food." Sporty patted his frail thigh as he laughed and joked.

"Yeah youngblood, them gators will love that tasty muthafucka. 'Cause she is finger-lickin good." They both exploded in laughter, then seconds later, Ray Ray's fatherly instinct kicked in when he noticed his son squirming irritably in his sleep from the sudden wave of noise.

"Shhhhh, we gotta' hold it down Sporty. I forgot my lil guy was sleep."

"I can dig it man," whispered Sporty. Ray Ray looked

toward the bathroom belligerently.

"Man I wonder what's takin' that dizzy broad so long."

"Ain't no tellin' youngblood, you know broads. And like I said befoe; that's one broad I do not trust."

The team of federal agents roamed throughout Syann's house fifteen minutes after they'd raided it. They searched for clues that coincided with the information that Smitty Branch had given them. And as a precaution, they had the entire area closed off within a ten-block radius. Special Agent Burns cracked a few corny jokes among his co-workers, then instructed two of the younger field-agents to go to Receiving Hospital to question Mr. Branch again. Meanwhile, they pretended to look for something specific, but was mainly snoopin' through Syann's portfolio of exotic photos that they'd found.

"Damn this bitch is gorgeous," sighed one of the white agents as he cuffed his crotch and spat a glob of spit-filled skoal on her floor. The rest of them all nodded in unison and continued to fantasize about the exploitation of every inch of her beautiful anatomy.

Mr. Branch moaned, wiggled, and mumbled as he impatiently waited for the anesthesia to kick in. He felt like he had finally made it to the hell that's described in various religious books, and the devil wasn't having any mercy. The nurses and doctors worked diligently to stabilize him for the necessary surgery to his third-degree burns. And as he finally began to slip under from the powerful anesthetic, the only thing that kept his spirits in perspective was the doctor's assurance to him that he'd live from his wounds.... The team of surgeons immediately began slicing thin layers of skin from various parts of his body, to graph more layers over his scorched face. They even had to resort to getting a dark-brown pig to graph skin from for the burns... It was an eleven-hour process.

CHAPTER 20

Thirty minutes after Syann dropped lil Ray off over her cousin's house, she pulled up at the heavily populated club in her money-green RX 330 Lexus truck.. Ray Ray and Sporty pulled up seconds behind her. When Syann parked and stepped from the truck, a few player-type dudes that had just climbed from a shiny black vette with Lambrogini doors, instantly made flirtatious gestures at her. The driver of the vette hissed and replied,

"Goddamn baby don't be so mean. I definitely need to be pullin' off with you on my passenger side tonight, real talk." Syann acknowledged the man with a simple smile but kept her runway stride movin' as her strapless lime-green Dolce & Gabbana dress complimented her every curve. Her ass shook and jiggled wickedly as she made her way to the entrance. Sporty shook his head as he watched her work the four-inch stilettos and run a hand through her shiny black latin-textured hair. Ray Ray irritably pulled out his cellphone and tried Sheila's number again. He hung up frustrated after a few tries with no answer. As he proceeded toward the front entrance with Sporty, he shared a personal thought out-loud.

"Man, I hope that bitch ain't puttin' me on a nigga wit' shoe-box money." Sporty smirked and nodded in agreement as they made their way through the front door.

"Hey beautiful, I thought you was gon' stand me up," said the man who slipped a hand around Syann's small waist.

He flashed a manish smile and rubbed his other hand over his 1980 Special-Ed type haircut.... The moment Syann frowned, is the exact moment the Cristal bottle came crashing down over dude's head... Tssshh!!

"Why da' fuck you got yo' hands all over my date nigga!" barked Lane. The man mumbled a ho-ish

"My fault Lane, I ain't know man." Then staggered to the otherside of the club. Lane nodded to the DJ and the bouncers to let them know everything was alright, then vagrantly turned his attention to Syann.

"Damn baby, you gon' let a nigga take my place that quick 'cause I'm five minutes late." Lane accused in a joking manner.

"Stop playin' baby, you know he ain't even my type. And it's a good thing that you got here when you did, 'cause I was 'bout to clock that fool myself. Puttin' his damn hands all on me like he know me or somethin. Anyway, whassup fa' da' night dark-n-lovely?" Syann ran a hand across his dark razor-bumped face suggestingly.

Lane was one of those brothers who looked like he was the missing link between man and ape. His skin was rough, he stood about 6'3, and he wore a bald head. He always pretended to be flattered when Syann would throw her bullshit compliments his way, because he knew he was a goolie-lookin mutha... But overall, he appreciated her sleazy tactics, because after all of the-

"*You so cute's, your skin so smooth, your teeth so white, and your lips so sexy,*" he would always take it out on her in the bedroom.

Lane was a major player in the narcotics trade, and he earned a solid dose of respect from most of the cats who knew him. Syann dug his style, because he was a good trick, and she enjoyed watchin' him think he was the livest nigga in Detroit. At one point, she almost thought he was just as gangsta as Ray Ray, until she really analyzed his credibility and compared the two. The streets were always watching, therefore, it would be the streets that declared who was who and to what degree. Lane had pull and could always get his point across effectively. But unlike Ray Ray, he had one major weakness. A phat ass and a cute smile. And was always willing to pay for pleasures of the flesh. Men like Lane were destined to fail. Ray Ray was driven by a different motivation. The methods to his madness was personal, which allowed him to remain discipline to his logic. And most of the top dawgs in the streets who would try to hold on to the little power that they'd accumulated over the years, would always let it be known that they respected Ray Ray... When in all actuality, they feared him. And the level of primacy he'd risen too, only instilled more fear.

Ballers, wanna-be-ballers, and sack-chasers danced and socialized to the good music in the club. Syann and Lane were fully in tune with the atmosphere as they laughed, partied, and had plenty drinks. Just as Lane was leading her to the floor for another dance, he was interrupted when a high-yellow man approached them and whispered in his ear... Lane displayed a look of surprise as he softly clutched the side of his head as if he'd forgotten something. He sleekly turned to Syann and gave a brief explanation.

"Check this out baby, I gotta' go handle some important business that I completely forgot about. So we'a get up with each other another day, a'ight."

Syann pouted as if she was disappointed, then put her spellbinding charm in full effect as she toyed with the button on his Armani shirt.

"Aw daddy, I was hoping we could spend some quality time together tonight. I had a lot of ex-," she paused for a moment and giggled to give off the teasing effect that was intended...

"Exotic fruits and whip cream that I wanted to experiment with tonight... Know what I mean. I was gonna' let you do a special taste-test." Lane raised a curious brow, then asked,

"Whatchu' mean taste-test baby?" He asked as he slid closer to her face.

Syann knew he loved to keep his long tongue buried deep in her pussy, so she licked her lips in a succulent manner. Then slid her hand underneath her dress, slipping two fingers in her slit. She twirled them around inside herself for thirty seconds then stopped... Moments later, she guided her cum-drenched fingers up to his mouth, then slowly pushed them inside... Lane didn't miss a beat as he sucked her fingers clean as if it was bar-b-que-sauce that dripped from a meaty steak.

"Mmm baby... Is that part of the taste test?" He asked with hungry lust in his eyes.

"Umm Hmm." She mouthed seductively.

"And the second part is covered with freshly squeezed strawberries. You ever had strawberry pussy baby?"

Lane shook his head no as if he was a LD-patient in a trance.

"Well, you will tonight. And I want you to be honest with me and tell me which one you liked the best, okay." She talked in a sultry tone. And to put the icing on the cake, she slowly slid off her matching G-string panties, and placed the balled-up garment in his hand.

"Hold on to these 'till I see you later, ok" She paused for half-a-second, then turned with grace and began walking away with her ass-cheeks applauding the room. Lane quickly grabbed her by the arm and pulled her close to his heaving chest.

"Come to think of it, I can handle this shit with you by my side, it won't take long, let's bounce."

Syann silently grinned to herself, because she knew exactly what it took for tender-dick-ass niggas like him to submit. She knew he couldn't stand the thought of her walking around a club full of lions, hot and bothered with no panties on. So once again, his weakness had caused him to violate another vital rule to the game. Remaining discipline to the sometimes toxic mix of business and pleasure.

Syann knew that Lane was the forgetful type. She'd been around him long enough to see the THC in the marijuana eat away at his memory glands. In the beginning, he would forget simple things like leaving a few thousand dollars in a pair of pants that ended up at the cleaners or forget to clean his 77-gallon fish tank, which would leave most of his exotic fish dead. But then it started getting worse. He would forget how much money a particular individual owed him, or how much product he'd passed out. And forget about important meetings with his connect, who saw it as nothing less than disrespect. Everyone around him began to take advantage of his slippin, and Syann knew it was just a matter of time before he was totally devoured by the wolves. She would always eat good off of him too, and on the strength of his potential, she more than once considered reforming him. But after giving it some serious thought, she concluded that sometimes you just can't teach an old dog new tricks. She would finally give him a taste of who she really was. She chose this night to hit his pockets hard because she remembered the important business at hand that he'd forgot about. Ray Ray smirked as Syann departed the club with Lane arm-in-arm.

Syann pulled up at the beautiful condo behind Lane's black 760 IL Beamer and hit the lights on her truck. Lane sat in the car for five minutes until three more vehicles pulled up. A black Range Rover, a silver Porsche Carrera GT. And a plain dark blue dodge caravan. They all stepped out as if on que and greeted Lane. Lane held up a hand to Syann and flashed five fingers twice to let her know he would be out in ten minutes. The two lieutenants under his command along with the two nineteen-year-olds in the van unloaded eleven full garbage bags and carried them into the condo. Ten minutes later, they all came out and hopped in their rides going in separate directions.

Lane signaled for Syann to come in, and she startlingly turned away, hoping he didn't see her snort the second line of cocaine. She glanced in her pocket-mirror to check her nose, then got out the truck and went inside. Syann noted how Lane had never brought her to that particular spot before as she peered around the lavish condo and admired the layout. *"Lane had good taste in furniture,"* she thought to herself. The black and gold Italian living-room set blended well with the black and gold Versace drapes. Marble adorned the floors throughout the spacious rooms. And the full chef kitchen and sizeable bar left her with a tingly feeling inside.

"Make ya'self at home baby!" he yelled from the bathroom. She did just that, by pouring herself a shot of Cranberry Grey Goose. She sipped until the glass was empty, then quickly poured herself another.

Lane entered the room moments later wearing only blue silk shorts with a blue G-Unit tank-top. He pulled her close to him and nibbled on her ear then whispered.

"I'm ready for that taste-test, so take this shit off." Syann giggled as she allowed him to slowly undress her...

The green strapless dress gently slid down her curvature to the floor as Lane drooled over her luscious goods. He gently massaged her soft breasts and sucked on her beautiful face and neck with urgency. He guided her over to the plush couch and playfully pushed her backwards. Her naked body bounced a few times and she quickly rolled out of his way before his diving body descended towards hers. She giggled and strutted her stuff over to the bottle of Grey Goose again. She poured them both a drink, then strolled back over to him... He reached pass the outstretched glass and pulled her close to him.

"Wait a minute baby," she mouthed in a tickled voice almost spilling the drinks.

"Didn't you pick up the strawberries on the way here?"

"Yeah, I did."

"Well go get'em daddy, and let's see if yo taste-buds are workin' tonight."

Lane smiled at her comments, then hurried to the kitchen to get the strawberries.

When he returned, Syann had just removed her twirling finger from his drink.

Lane sat the bowl of strawberries on the glass table, then laid Syann down on the couch. He straddled her, then anxiously sucked and slobbed on her protruding nipples. He worked his way down to her moiste treasure, then slowly worked his tongue, in and around her open flesh... Syann rubbed his head as he continued to lick, then tilted her head back and enjoyed his lapping tongue... Five minutes later, she gently pushed his head up and handed him the glass of Grey Goose. Lane downed it then eagerly leaned toward her open flesh again, but she stopped him.

"Hold up baby. This good pussy ain't goin' nowhere, alright? Now it's time for the main event, so let's see if you'a contender or pretender." Syann reached over inside the bowl on the table and clutched a fist full of strawberries. She dropped a few on her flat stomach, then held the remaining ones over her exposed slit and squoze as hard as she could, creating a quick sticky flow of strawberry slush that ran down, in, and around her pussy and ass. She smeared the juice and broken pieces of strawberry all over her hole, then seductively began licking the contents off her wet, sticky fingers...

The whole scene drove Lane crazy, and he didn't waste any time licking every drop of juice or piece of fruit whenever he saw it, then licked and sucked on her pussy like a crazed animal... Syann wasn't really trying to enjoy the session as much as she normally would, due to the fact that this was a different level of business. But she had to admit to herself, his energetic tongue was feeling extremely good tonight, which is why she came twice within ten minutes...

As Lane continued to slurp her juices, he suddenly began to slow down and wipe his sweat-drenched face...

He displayed an irritated expression, and his eyes seemed to be blinking in slow-motion... Suddenly, he grabbed at his throat as he tasted small amounts of regurgitated strawberries. He aggressively began to massage near his adam's apple as his trachea began to tighten up, with more sweat pouring from his head... His eyesight became blurry and his equilibrium became overwhelmingly unsteady.

He suddenly realized that Syann had slipped something in his drink. And in that instance, he lunged toward her face, getting his hands fully gripped around her neck. The pressure he applied quickly went from intense to mild, and his eager hands gracefully lost its grasps as all the muscles in his body gave out... Syann quickly slid her naked body from under him, then ran and opened the front door for Ray Ray. When Ray Ray stepped in, his eyes briefly scanned her nakedness, then he attempted to brush pass her but she quickly grabbed his hand and pulled herself close to him.

She stared deeply in his eyes and gave an inviting gaze that clearly said, "*Take me however you want me.*" Her mouth hung slightly open, and her chest heaved deeply as the excited adrenaline rushed throughout her body. Her bothered loins begged to be touched, and she was totally submissive to whatever he desired.

Ray Ray snatched away from her, then strolled over to the couch where Lane laid on his back, barely conscious with his eyes hung low... Ray Ray stood in front of Lane and showed no remorse for the pathetic condition he was in. Then moments later, he calmly retrieved a glock 45 from his waist and aimed it at his head.

"Wait! Wait! Ray Ray!" Syann yelled frantically.

"He ain't no threat and he ain't goin' nowhere. I put

some potent shit in his Grey Goose. He can still talk, but I swear, he's otherwise outta' commission."

"Hold up man!" Lane's plea came a split-second after Syann's quick explanation.

"You ain't gotta-" Lane paused for a full seven seconds as his mind recollected where he remembered the familiar face from. It was about seven years ago when Ray Ray had invaded his mentor Big Dex's home and took eight-hundred thousand in cash, then executed him. Lane was just comin' up in the ranks at the time, and he was petrified as he hid in a basket full of dirty clothes listening to his street-teacher gurgle his last breath…. It was the legendary Ray Ray. And he couldn't believe he was back. A new level of fear gripped his body as he spoke-up nervously in a slurred voice.

"Man, please don't kill me, you can have everything in here. Just don-"

"Nigga cut all that pussy-ass whining out fo' I kill you on the strength nigga." Ray Ray scolded and aimed the gun toward him aggressively as he finished his statement.

"Don't kill'em Ray Ray, he gon' be sleepin' like a baby in a few minutes. And by the time he wake-up, we'a be long gone." Syann interjected again as she pulled the last portion of her dress up.

As Lane slowly slipped in and out of consciousness, he spoke out to Ray Ray again.

"Man damn, what did I do to make you hate me so much?"

Ray Ray smirked at him before answering.

"I don't hate you nigga… Hate would cloud my judgement. I just don't like you." Those were the last words Lane heard as the faded figure in front of him went blank.

Syann and Ray Ray checked the eleven garbage bags, which seven out of the eleven held money. The remaining bags held cocaine. Syann reached in one of the bags and playfully tossed Ray Ray a ten-thousand-dollar stack and stated,

"That's the ten G's I owe you from back in the day, now we even."

Ray Ray looked at her blankly with an unimpressed expression, then began loading the money in their vehicles with a nonchalant demeanor.

CHAPTER 21

As Ray Ray and Syann pulled up at the safe spot, he thought about how he let Syann talk him into letting Lane live, when normally it would've been curtains for his ass. Because Ray Ray knew it was always highly dangerous to let a mark live to see another day, despite how much he'd beg and plead for his life. He knew all to well from experience that it definitely ain't no fun when the rabbit got the gun...

After Syann, Sporty, and Ray Ray counted the 2.3 million with two different money machines, Ray Ray made a trip to the three different safety-deposit boxes he'd reserved. He distributed the money evenly in the three boxes and told Syann and Sporty that they would get a fair share when the mission was completely over.

Syann discreetly stashed the five kilos of cocaine that she managed to smuggle behind Ray Ray's back when they robbed Lane, then eagerly got herself prepared for the next caper.... Over the course of the next seven days, Ray Ray and Syann pulled off ten more scores, and accumulated an additional four-point-two million in cash. And only two people out of the ten licks that they hit, had to be murdered for tryna' be cowboys. Syann had successfully controlled the rest of them with her lethal combination of sedative slash seduction.

After another failed attempt at reaching Sheila, Ray

Ray cursed to himself and sunk back into the couch in a deep state of anguish. The fact that he hadn't talked to Sheila since he told her about his new son was eating him alive. And Syann was lovin' every minute of it because she felt that if Sheila continued to stay out of the picture, the better her chances would be with Ray Ray becoming her man. She glanced over at Ray Ray as he remained visibly irritated and bothered about Sheila and decided to help out with the situation. She did a couple lines of cocaine, then put in one of her favorite R-Kelly CD's and turned up the volume.

"When a Woman's fed up, there ain't nothing you can do about it, it's like runnin' outta' luck, and it's too late to talk about it." Ray Ray looked up angrily when he heard the song, and immediately yelled for Syann to cut it off... She now had her back to him with a smirk on her face, acting as if she didn't hear him.

"Ay!" he yelled again.

"Turn dat shit off!"

Syann held fast as she continued to pop her fingers and play deaf... Until one of Ray Ray's airforce one's came crashing into the back of her left shoulder.

"Ouuw Ray Ray. What da' hell wrong wit' you?" She played dumb.

"I said turn dat shit off, now!"

"But that's one of my favorite cuts Ray Ray."

"Girl, I don't give a fuck what it is, now turn it the fuck off and put something else on."

"Somethin' else like what Ray Ray?"

"Somethin' else like I'll beat dat bitch wit' a bat! Live and in concert if you don't stop playin wit me hoe!"

Syann instantly got wet between her legs at the thought of how she'd just got under his skin, then turned it off altogether and strolled to another room...

****

After Lane concluded his meeting with most of the top dealers in the city, he turned his attention toward the group of hungry goons that occupied the room. He'd called upon them for assistance because they thirsted for drama every chance they got. Especially for the almighty dolla... After Lane offered up twenty-five thousand for Ray Ray's head, one of the lil dudes in the crowd known as Von suddenly blurted out,

"You say this nigga Ray Ray thorough huh?"

Everyone in the room instantly focused on Von.

"Yeah." Answered Lane, while eyeing the youngsta intently.

"The most thorough you ever seen, right?"

"Yeah, you could say that." Lane answered again, slightly confused, not really knowing where Von's head was at.

"And you say you want the nigga's life?"

Screwfaced and charged about the youngsta's line of questioning, Lane answered sternly.

"Hell fuck yeah lil nigga. That's what I want."

"Then it's fifty playa." Shouted Von.

No-one said a word, including Lane as the youngsta's audacious, but logical remark floated through the room.

He was playing purely off the level of fear that danced in Lane's eyes for Ray Ray. *"This pussy nigga scared to death."* Von thought to himself as he waited for a response.

After a few moments of silence, they all turned to Lane to see if he would honor the youngsta's ticket. Then he spoke up.

"A'ight, I'll tell you what gangsta. Since you talkin' like

you cut like that, gimee a brief spill of yo' resume' in the business of disposal, and we'a go from there."

Von smirked at Lane's remark then spoke matter-of-factly.

"Resume, Hmph. Man check this out. Do you remember them Best-Friend niggas that had niggas shook the fuck up around here for awhile?" Von continued before Lane could answer.

"Or them Chambers boys and YBI niggas?"

Lane raised a brow and eagerly chimed,

"Yeah." Anxious to hear what Von had to say about the players he'd just named.

"Well let's just say I penetrated they forces in one way or another, and put a few thrillers down on some of they top-dawgs sumthin scandalous, ya feel me?" He winked when he concluded his statement, and stood there with a *"Im da' shit"* expression.

Everyone in the room suddenly focused on the youngsta with a new-found respect for him... Everyone except Lane because he peeped that Von was lying. He was way too young to have been in the mix when those crews rained supreme throughout the city. But Lane liked the lil peanut-head nigga's spunk, so he decided to give him a shot at becoming the exaggerated legend he claimed to be....

"He just might fuck around and pull it off." Lane thought to himself. Then he doled out petty cash to several different stragglers in the room who claimed they knew a friend of a friend, who was sexing a baby-mama's cousin, who in turn kicked it with Ray Ray all the time. Lane didn't believe half the stories they was shootin' at him, but he didn't care because he figured it like this, if five out of fifteen of the stories happen to check out, it would

be five more chances to the good for his problem. And aside from that, the few fifteen-hundred-dollar payoff's he dished out here and there was a long way from hurting his pockets. The only real burden for him at this point was the fact that his connect had eventually started puttin' pressure on him about the loss of their money. So Lane in turn had to start puttin' pressure on the people who said they could neutralize Ray Ray... He offered an additional fifteen Gs for the death of Syann as well.

CHAPTER 22

Ray Ray spoke in a low whisper as he sat down beside Sporty on the couch and leaned toward his ear.

"Peep this Sporty. That bitch been actin' a little suspect lately and I don't like it. So what I'ma do is take the bitch to the mall, and I want you to search this muthafucka thoroughly for anything outta' the ordinary while we gone, a'ight?"

"A'ight baby-boy, I gotchu. I'ma turn this muhfucka upside down, 'cause I know that bitch ain't right."

Syann came out the bathroom with a suspicious expression just as Sporty finished his statement. She noticed the skeptical looks on their faces, then briskly opened her hands and shrugged her shoulders.

"What?" She asked defensively... Neither Sporty or Ray Ray answered.

Twenty minutes later, Ray Ray and Syann were strolling through the mall with a few different bags of purchased clothes in tow. They visited several department stores and accumulated several more clothes and shoes. Ray Ray bought his son an entire new wardrobe and picked up five plush multi-colored Pelle's for himself. They had to take the first load of items to the car, in order to be able to carry the things that they'd purchase on the second round. Ray Ray wanted to give Sporty sufficient time to search the house, so he let Syann flex a few notches harder than women normally did when it came to shopping.

Their final stop was the woman's footlocker. Ray Ray found the young girl behind the cash register amusing as she discussed different discounts with Syann yet kept a trained eye on him the entire time. Her peanut-butter complexion, corn rows and underdeveloped body made her appear to be more innocent and fragile than she probably was. She was nomore than eighteen, but the way she over-pronounced the word *"Yes"* whenever it was called for, and occasionally licked her lips and batted her eyes at Ray Ray, made her look a few years beyond her age.

Syann caught the advances she was making, then calmly leaned within earshot of her as they concluded their business and whispered.

"He's not for you honey, 'cause number one, he's not into little girls. And number two, he's a thug."

"OOWW" responded the girl quickly.

"They say never judge a book by its cover, and uh, he looks more like a gangster to me boo." She voiced in her best impersonation of an uppity white girl.

Syann eyed the teenager as if she wanted to slap the sassy remark from her mouth, but instead, she would settle for getting the last word.

"Let me tell you somethin' little girl, you better get'chu some bidness befoe' I give you the kind that I truly don't think you ready for." Syann's eyes and posture dared the girl to retaliate. But after a few seconds of contemplation, the girl just rolled her eyes and released a muffled "humph."

Satisfied with the girl's cop-out, Syann mouthed "I thought so" as she walked out with the five boxes of shoes she'd just purchased.

After about three steps into the common area of the mall, the loud whack! Caused Ray Ray to suddenly look back. Whack! Whack! Whack!

"Bitch! I-knew –I –was –gon' –see –yo' –bitch-ass again!" yelled the tall darkskinned man as he landed blow after blow to Syann's face... Syann dropped the bags as she tried to shield herself from the continuous blows that rained on her relentlessly.

"Four hundred thousand bitch! I want my money! You betta' come up with my shit!" ..Plack! –Plack!

"Aahgg." Suddenly the man was on the floor trying to shield himself from the two quick blows from the 45 automatic that knocked him silly. Plack! Ray Ray brutally slammed the pistol over the top of his head as blood skeeted from the fresh open gashes.

"I took yo' money nigga! Now act like you want it back."

Plack! The man attempted to run but his weakened body wouldn't obey his eager mind.

Syann slipped off one of her stilettos and slammed it into the side of his left jaw. He shrieked out as the pointed heel lodged in his face.

"You punk muthafucka! How do it feel, huh?" Syann spat as she enjoyed the extra pain she'd just inflicted.

Ray Ray aimed the gun at his head and was about to put him out of his misery until Syann yelled

"No Ray Ray!" then pointed at the mall security-guard that was approaching them fast. With his walkie-talkie nervously pressed to his mouth, and his hand gripped tightly on his unholstered weapon...

When the black bulky guard got within' preferred range, he yelled "Drop the weapon and place your hands above your head. Now!" Ray Ray smirked at the toy cop, then slapped his already bloody victim across the head again.

"I bet you won't rape another woman you piece'a shit." He yelled loud enough for the guard to hear him, and Syann immediately picked up on Ray Ray's pitch. She suddenly ran towards the guard with her hands in the air pleading.

"He raped me! He raped me!"

"Get back lady, now!" yelled the trembling guard.

"No No, you don't understand, he raped me in the bathroom of your mall, and my husband is giving him just what he deserves." Syann's words somewhat softened the guard's demeanor, but he still kept the gun trained on her as she submissively inched her way within his space.

Suddenly, Syann dropped to her knees directly in front of him, bawling like a spanked child. She covered both of her eyes as she pretended to be in total distress about the entire situation, then bent forward as her sobs became louder.

Ray Ray's victim instantly began to glance around with a confused expression when he kept hearing the word rape tossed around in reference to him. And just when he was about to speak up in his own defense, Ray Ray slapped him hard across his head again.... The guard demanded Ray Ray to put the gun down as he aimed aggressively and sweated profusely. Syann kept on with her role as she continuously sobbed and rocked at his feet.

Ray Ray knew it would only be a matter of seconds before the other guards would show up, possibly with the police. So he knew he had to create a way to get up outta' there fast...

Syann, seeming to have read his thoughts, suddenly did the unexpected. She reached upward toward the guard with lightening speed, and got a firm grip on his weapon... As they tussled and fought for control of the gun, Ray Ray dashed over to them and knocked the guard over the head with his 45... The guard stumbled backwards but didn't fall, so Ray Ray didn't waste any time whackin him again. This time he dropped to the floor in a slumber as he went out cold.

Ray Ray and Syann instantly took flight, leaving all of their purchased items behind. They ran hard and fast, barely making it pass the back-up security that was now on the scene. They maneuvered their way throughout the building until they finally came to an exit...

"Hey! You two!" yelled one of the security-guards just as they were bounding through the door... The frail black guard had his weapon drew and yelled again frantically as he desperately tried to get his point across. Ray Ray calmly turned toward the guard with a blank expression and raised his weapon in a care-free fashion. Boh! Boh! Boh! Boh! Boh!

The toy-cop wasn't hit by any of the slugs, but he still laid curled up on the floor in the fetal position shaking like a leaf on a windy day as Ray Ray and Syann made a clean getaway.

As Ray Ray and Syann made it within seven blocks of the safe-house, Syann broke the silence.

"I can't believe that punk-ass Tim tried to get at me like that. I shoulda' let you kill the nigga when we got his ass for that paper."

Syann took a few minutes to process all the information she'd just spoke on, then spoke up again.

"Ray Ray, let me ask you something."

"What?" he answered dryly.

"Through all the bullshit, how do you always stay so

mentally grounded?" Ray Ray took a few moments before he answered, then spoke up as her question caused him to reflect on the true stability to his sanity.

"Cause number one, I never, ever forget the pain. And number two, I know that war is a part of every free man's creed. Cut and dry."

Syann felt that her question couldn't have been answered any better. She pondered on his words momentarily and absorbed every ounce of the euphoric effect it sent through her system. She suddenly felt as if she was in love all over again, and for the first time in her life, it hurt so good.

After a few moments of enjoying the rush, she exhaled deeply then responded.

"Ray Ray, despite all that we've been through, I just want you to know that I've never met a man who moved me the way you do. And regardless of how things may play out wit' us, you've definitely left an everlasting impression in my life. I put that on everything I love."

Ray Ray didn't give her the kind of response she'd hoped for. He seemed totally unmoved by her words. He didn't flinch, change facial expressions, or utter a word during the rest of their short trip.

Ray Ray made a quick stop at the spy-shop on the way. He ran in and came back out a few seconds later with a small brown paper-bag in hand... They arrived at the safe-house twenty minutes later.

CHAPTER 23

Special Agent Burns took another sip of his black coffee before giving Agent Barker the feedback he waited for.

"The ball is definitely in our court now, so hold fast and let's see what happens."

"Do you honestly think it's gonna workout partner?" asked Agent Barker curiously.

"At this point, I truly have no reason to think otherwise. Like I said before, we have the advantage right now..." Agent Burns smirked before finishing his statement.

"Some people fortunately leave everlasting impressions on others." They both laughed as they sipped their coffee....

****

When Ray Ray and Syann walked through the front door, the first thing they saw was Sporty sitting on the couch in front of a table with most of the contents from Syann's purse scattered about. There was a Nextel cellphone, a couple boxes of condoms, tampons, loose change, a box cutter, and two kilos of cocaine.

Sporty wore a proud look on his face because he felt good about what he accomplished on his mission. He took a long drag from the Kool cigarette before giving Ray Ray a verbal explanation on his findings.

"Check it out youngblood. I found most of this shit in one of the bitch purses, but the coke was hid in one of her shoeboxes deep in the closet of her room. I didn't find nothing else, but this here is credible enough to applaud our suspicion's ya dig. In a nutshell, the bitch ain't shit."

"Fuck you nigga!" she barked. "Who da' fuck is you to be passin' judgement on somebody as fucked up as you is? And you ain't have no muthafuckin bidness goin' thru my shit either nigga!"

"Shut da' fuck up bitch! Just shut up." Ray Ray snarled as he looked at her with a dogmatic stare.

"What da' fuck else you hidin' bitch, huh? Whutchu be doin' with dat shit, sellin' it or usin' it?"

Syann didn't wanna answer the question, so she looked away in an attempt to avoid it altogether....

"Bitch! I asked you a question, is you sellin- or usin!" Ray Ray asked again scornfully. And it was clearly understood that his anger had elevated a few notches.

Syann was more than uncomfortable with his line of questioning, but she knew she had to face her biggest demon sooner or later. So she closed her eyes tightly and let the overflow of tears burst through freely as she mumbled her answer.

"Using Ray Ray, alright. I'm usin."

Ray Ray shook his head negatively then shouted.

"You stupid bitch! How you gon' raise a baby usin' that shit! Huh? Damn. I'm sick of bein' around so many weak-minded muthafuckas. You of all people should know that shit ain't 'bout nothing. And it don't do nothin' but put flaws in an otherwise airtight game. That's one of the easiest ways for the muthafuckin' feds to get control of a muthafucka's mind and pick'em for everything they know. It's a-" Ray Ray paused for a moment as he thought about his last statement. Then suddenly demanded her to sit down on the couch next to Sporty.

"Stay Put!" he squawked, then ran to his bedroom in a hurry...

Agent Burns smiled as he sat in the white low-key Dodge van and spoke over the walkie-talkie.

"That's a ten-four comrade. I have one in position with the suspect, and it's almost time to move." ....

****

When Ray Ray returned from his bedroom, he walked toward the couch with a grimacing expression. Syann's stomach did flips and she began to perspire as he came within inches of her... Suddenly, she submissively threw her hands up and yelled

"No Ray Ray! No!" as he retrieved the chrome 45 from his waist...aimed and fired. Boh!

Aahgg!" She screamed and closed her eyes as she braced herself for the pain she knew was destined to come.

Suddenly, she opened her eyes and instantly became confused when she saw the large hole in Sporty's chest... Ray Ray immediately stood over him the moment he dropped to the floor. He leaned over Sporty and aggressively snatched his shirt open, then shook his head negatively when he saw the taped-up wire snaked across his chest and torso.

A lump formed in his throat, and he fought desperately to hold back his tears as he shouted.

"You see this Sporty! Huh? You see this!" He held up the device that closely resembled a beeper as he explained.

"It's called a de-bugger muthafucka! It vibrates whenever a bug is within eight feet of it." Ray Ray turned his head in a squirm-like manner, as if the whole ordeal was too deeply under his skin. Then he suddenly reached down and ripped the wire off and calculated how much time he had left, down to the seconds before the goons would come.

"Sporty you was the main nigga always talkin' 'bout how you hated snitches... When did you go wrong man, and why?"

Sporty hesitated on giving a response as he grunted from the lodged bullet in his chest.

"Ba- Baby-boy, the store that you helped me get off the ground, tur- turned out to be more of a curse more-so than a gift. You- you know how it is wit' us, we see opportunity, and we jump on it. Man I saw an opportunity to get more paper on the tax side of thangs. An- and the feds fucked around and hit me wit' tax-evasion. They was talkin' life off the top 'cause this trip officially made me a habitual offender. I couldn't see myself goin' out like that so I played ball. At first all they wanted you for was givin' me the ten G's to start the business. But onc- aggh."

The pain began to take a toll on him, and he took a few seconds to continue.

"Once they found out who you really was, they offered me a prison-free pass and put that same ten back in my pocket. They knew that me and your father was tight and they pressed... It was bigger than me baby-boy, I swear."

A quote from Jadakiss instantly popped in Ray Ray's mind.

"Why is rattin at an all-time high?"

"Damn Sporty." He sighed.

"I thought you was among the last breed of gangsta's. My father doin' flips in his grave right now. You managed to fuck up real good this time Sporty. You broke my heart man." Boh! ...The single bullet tore through Sporty's skull, leaving him lifeless with a shocked facial expression... Then after a few seconds of watching his corpse, he suddenly snapped out of it and yelled

"Come on Syann! Run, hurry up! Hurry up!"

"All units go! go! go!"

Syann and Ray Ray dashed toward the Audi A-8 in a hurry, but Ray Ray quickly retracted their path when he realized Sporty also had the Audi bugged. They jumped in Syann's Lexus truck, and it chirped forward with the tires squealing as Ray Ray mashed hard on the gas. The moment they made it to the corner, the plain white police van attempted to block them off, but Ray Ray skillfully maneuvered the truck around them and skidded off wildly.

Before he could make it completely off the block, two burgundy Crown Victoria's and three blue and white police cars appeared seemingly out of nowhere... They instantly heated up the pursuit. Syann adjusted her seatbelt and sat there with a worried expression as Ray Ray drove hard and fast. He suddenly yanked the wheel to the left, making a sharp turn to avoid a vicious collision with a sky-blue neon, then zoomed down Harper as fast as the truck would go. The police drove just as reckless and wouldn't seem to let up despite the many near-accidents Ray Ray caused in an attempt to lose them.

Ray Ray bust a quick right on chalmers, then gunned the truck full speed. He wished he would've been in the Audi instead, because he felt his chances of losing them would've been a lot of horse-powers better. As the chase advanced, Ray Ray noticed more police cars coming from different side-streets attempting to block him in. But they would always seem to be a few seconds too late, and he'd swerve right around them.

"Syann!" he called out as he navigated the truck through the heavy traffic.

"Check this out. If I gotta' bail up out this muhfucka on foot, don't say nothin' to them bitches about nothin' when they arrest you. Just sit tight and I'll be to get you out on bond. A'ight."

Syann agreed as her body leaned, rocked, and jerked from the rough ride.

Just as Ray Ray made it to Chalmers and Warren, the Lexus locked its brakes and slung around the corner. He was momentarily out of sight, then ten seconds later, he jerked the wheel and slammed on the brakes hard to avoid hitting the two patrol cars that blocked his path. The Lexus made a full spin, creating a hail of smoke from the squealing tires, then sped down Warren in the opposite direction. Ray Ray bust another left on Lakeview, then gunned it down the narrow street... He ended up on Kercherval and Marlborough five minutes later. And just as he made it to the corner of Ashland, all four of the tires on the Lexus truck blew out as he drove over the razor-sharp spike-strips that the police had put down.

"Damn!" he shouted as the truck swerved and slammed into a huge pole. Ray Ray knew in his heart that he wasn't trying to go to prison, 'cause to him, incarceration was just one step above death.

He didn't waste any time bailing out and running through a few vacant lots and jumping a few gates before he was able to flag down a cab and get out of harms way... It seemed as if fifty law-enforcement officials had guns eagerly drawn on Syann as she sat there with her hands held high trying not to make the slightest move. They aggressively snatched her from the truck, then put the handcuffs on extra tight as they strong-armed her into the backseat of one of their vehicle's and combed the area for Ray Ray...

CHAPTER 24

The dark complected elderly woman's face became aglow as she hurriedly put the remainder of collard-greens in her shopping cart... She rushed her unsteady body over to the light-skinned police officer and nervously pointed her finger in the opposite direction as she explained her issue... Moments later, the uniformed officer now wore the same facial expression as the silver-haired woman, as he anxiously trudged toward the person she'd just pointed at.... Suddenly, his target dipped behind an aisle. Which caused him to speed up, then slow down in a low crouch with his 7mm glock now gripped tightly in his hand. As he cautiously inched his way around the back of the aisle and waved shoppers out of his line of fire, he grabbed his walkie-talkie and decided to call for back-up before the situation got out of hand...

But just as he pressed the button, the barrel of the 380 Ruger sunk firmly against his temple.

"I wouldn't do that if I were you. Wouldn't wanna mess up that nice haircut of yours, now would we?" Sheila hissed in an icy tone as she calmly took control of the situation. The officer sighed and felt defeated as she snatched his weapon from his hand and demanded him to walk toward the front door.

Many of the people in the store cringed and frantically moved out of the way as they made their way to the exit. Sheila stopped abruptly at the elderly woman who'd alerted the police to her presence. She hauled off and slapped the old woman with the pistol and chimed,

"Next time you see a wanted bitch, mind ya damn business granny. You are entirely too old for that bullshit."

The woman's body flung backwards, and she toppled to the floor hard. Her glasses went one way, and her false teeth went another.... The woman had noticed Sheila in the store and remembered her from the Michigan's Most Wanted segments. That's when she'd alerted the officer who was now being held at gunpoint.

As they made it through the front door, they approached the officer's squad-car. Sheila calmly tapped the passenger window to alert the other black officer to the situation. As he looked up, his face showed surprise when he saw her with the gun to his partner's head. He anxiously looked as if he wanted to make a heroic move to turn things in his favor, but Sheila quickly blurted,

"Don't be a hero pig, you can't win. Now step out!" she demanded.... The officer hesitated before complying to her demand, until a slight nod from his partner caused him to do as he was told.

When he stepped out, Sheila retrieved his weapon, then pushed the other officer beside him. As they stood there, she politely ordered them to stay put while she reached inside the car and popped their trunk.

"Okay gentlemen, I'd like you to take one pair of cuffs, and cuff yourselves together. But don't make it too tight, 'cause I want yall to learn from this."

The officers displayed pitiful expressions as they cuffed themselves together.

"Now, I want you both to climb in that trunk and make

ya'selves nice and cozy."

"Come on lady, you already got us subdued. Just make your getaway and leave us here 'til help comes, alright."

Sheila instantly cocked her weapon as a sign of her displeasure with the high-yellow officer's remark.

"We can do this the easy way, or the hard way. Make your choice pig."

The outspoken officer pouted like an elementary student not having his way. Then reluctantly began to climb into the trunk.

As he fumbled around trying to occupy the crampy space and balance himself with his cuffed hand and free hand, his partner stood there and patiently waited for his turn to step inside the trunk.

A few moments later, he lifted his left leg and placed it in the trunk. And just as he appeared to be lifting his other one, he suddenly leaned downward in a flash and gripped the backup pistol in his ankle holster. But before he could come up with it, Boh! Boh! The two sporadic shots from Sheila buckled him and caused him to slump over in the trunk in a wild manner. The shots she discharged caught him around his right hamstring and just above the area of his right kidney.

"You stupid muthafucka! What's wrong with you. It always gotta' be a hero out the bunch, so I guess you him huh?" She strolled over to him as he moaned in pain, then pushed the rest of his body into the trunk on top of his frightened partner.

"I'm not usually a violent person, but stupid shit like this brings the bitch up outta' me everytime. Now my advice to you is, don't be so damn stupid next time." She slammed the trunk shut and pulled off in the burgundy rented Toyota Camry seconds later.

As Sheila drove through the city of Detroit, she reflected back on some of the literature she'd read while she was incarcerated. She particularly found herself reading more and more of the Prince Machiavelli because his logic and approach was always practical and sensible to her. And at this point, her present life seemed to help her understand some of the principles and philosophies of the prince. And the more she studied him, the more she saw a lot of his ways and tactics instilled in Ray Ray. Mainly the one that says *"It's far more better to be feared than loved if you cannot be both."*

Sheila navigated her way through the city in deep thought, and she mumbled quotes from Niccoli Machiavelli aloud as if she was practicing for a broadway play.

"A wise person will rely on what he controls, not on what he cannot control. And he must know how to act according to the nature of half-man, half-beast, fore he can not survive otherwise.... A prince should not deviate from what is good if that is possible. But he should know how to do evil if that is necessary." She smiled to herself before reciting the last quote. *"Everyone sees what you appear to be. Few experience what you really are."*

****

As Von sat in the black old-school cutlass under the dimly lit street-light, he smiled to himself as he reflected on the day's events. He thought about how it was undoubtedly in his favor to be at the mall today when all the drama jumped off with Ray Ray and Syann, because it gave him the edge he needed for the situation at hand. He'd already knew what Syann looked like because his uncle use to trick with her from time to time. And he never forgot her face because he use to fantasize about sexin her fine ass someday himself.

As for Ray Ray, his face had been flashed on the crime-stoppers program so many times, that it was hard to forget his face too. Von had followed Syann and Ray Ray back to the safe house, but before he could make his move, the high-speed chase ensued. He joined in on the chase but drove as cautiously as he could without raising any suspicion to his vehicle. He stayed a safe distance behind the police cars as they drove recklessly through traffic. And even though he badly wanted to assassinate Ray Ray, he still had to admire his driving ability. And all throughout the chase, he prayed that Ray Ray would get away.

Von had panicked momentarily when the cops that followed Ray Ray lost him for a brief spell, because if Ray Ray were to get away, he had no clues as to where he might go. And the fifty-thousand-dollar ticket on his head would more than likely go uncollected... But after a few moments of scanning the area with Ray Ray nowhere in sight, Von had became hopeful again when he noticed Ray Ray flag down a cab and jump in... Von followed the cab to Ray Ray's back-up safe house, then sat outside in his cutty and waited for his moment.

As Von sat there and continued to reflect, he didn't feel the slightest bit of remorse for the teenage boy he'd ran over during the chase. He smirked to himself as he thought about how he peered through the rearview mirror after hitting the boy, and witnessed several other cars roll over his body before they could stop.

Von took another pull from the neatly rolled blunt he held, then reclined in his seat until he felt it was showtime.

After making it inside the safe house in one piece, Ray Ray immediately changed clothes and peeped out the window every five minutes like a paranoid crackhead. He had several weapons laid out around him in case the police somehow found his hideout. After a couple hours went by, his nerves calmed a bit and he moved less anxiously throughout the house. He decided to take a shower, then try Sheila's phone again afterwards because he was dying to get back in good graces with her. It was difficult for him to think clearly, and he felt empty without her....

Just as he was about to step into the shower, his cellphone rung. He hesitated before answering it because he didn't recognize the number.... After about seven rings, he answered.

"Hello."

"Is this Ray Ray?" the female caller asked.

"Who is this?" he asked defensively.

"This is Syann's cousin Oeekwa. The one who's been keepin' lil Ray for her."

"Oh..Whassup?"

"Syann called me a minute ago and said she don't know how she got a bond this fast, but she got one and she tryna' be up outta there A.S.A.P"

"A'ight, that's straight. How much is it?"

"Twenty thousand at ten percent."

Ray Ray quickly scribbled the amount on a piece of paper, then focused back on the caller.

"A'ight, check it out. I'ma get witchu the first thing tomorrow Oeekwa. And you can go scoop her up, a'ight."

"Okay Ray Ray...And oh, I almost forgot. I don't know if Syann told you or not, but I'm the one who handled the cremation situation for ya boy Smoke. Syann told me how you wanted it done, so I pretended like I was one of his closest family members. And after a little harassment and a bunch of questions, they let me pay, get it done, and bring his ashes home in a crystal vase that I picked out. So, when I see you tomorrow, I got that for you, ok?"

Ray Ray instantly found himself on an emotional roller-coaster all over again as the reality of Smoke's fate body-slammed his heart. He struggled to find a response, but long seconds of silence filled the phone. Oeekwa sensed he was still in deep grievance over his friend. And judging from his character, she also figured he appreciated what she'd done. So in that regard, she let her mind hear the silent *"Thank You"* that never left Ray Ray's mouth, then calmly replied

"Your welcome Ray Ray. I'll see you in the morning." The phone went dead as he sat there with a distraught expression, wishing it was all a dream.... He managed to come out of his trance about ten minutes later, then stepped in the shower and let the extra-warm water assist him with the relaxation he was badly in need of.

Meanwhile, Von was now out of his car and on the side of the house discreetly stooped low beside a window. He eased up above the windowsill and peered through in hopes of seeing Ray Ray, but due to the tightly closed blinds, he couldn't see anything.

He crouched low and moved in a sneaky stride to another window, then waited a few seconds before peeking through.

"Damn." He whispered to himself when he wasn't able to see inside of that one either, so he repositioned himself, paused for a moment until the car with the bright headlights passed by, then didn't waste any time heading to another window...

"Fuck!" he cursed when another set of closed blinds wouldn't accommodate him in his efforts. He pulled out the 40-caliber pistol, looked it over, then said to himself

"Fuck it. I'ma just have to go guerilla-style up in that muhfucka. Kick the goddamn door off the hinges and slump this nigga." He smiled to himself at the thought of not only getting the fifty G's, but he would be legendary in the streets. And with that status alone, he could press soft niggas like Lane for more dough, as well as keep a solid plug on a good quality of cocaine. His heart thumped in his chest rapidly as he became more excited about all that he was about to accomplish. And he was more than ready to put it down as he mumbled lyrics from his favorite rapper Duce Cannon. *"I'd rather be the nigga behind the trigga, instead of bein' the nigga wit the twisted figure/so when it's time I'ma let the 40-cal bust, the hood cold and it taught me not to ever trust."*

He pulled hard on the top-half of the pistol, then immediately let it go. As it sprung back in place, the bullet that was now in the chamber gave him an adrenaline rush as he made his way back toward the front of the house... He squatted low again when he made it a few feet away from the porch, then scanned the area once more to make sure nobody was around.

He eased up slowly, almost in an upright position as he prepared to make his move... Then suddenly, he thought he was losing his mind when he felt the hard object pressed firmly against the back of his peanut-shaped head.

"One of the common flaws of mankind is, they never

anticipate a storm when the sea is calm. Are you here to kill my husband?" Sheila asked as she held the black 380 tightly against his head.

"Na- Naw, I- I wasn't 'bout to kill nobody." Von lied as he explained nervously.

"Well, the bad news about this situation is, I think you're a big liar. And in situations like this, you should be trying to come up with a reasonable contingency plan instead of lying."

"Wha- what do you mean?" Von stammered.

"I mean, like begging for your life for starters. Now go'head, let me hear you beg for your life."

Von hesitated before mumbling,

"What's the point."

"The point is, despite what happens, you at least gave yourself a chance. Because your assailant just might have a soft spot somewhere at heart. And if your begging creates any empathy, you just might live to play another day. Now give ya'self a chance and Bitch-up guy."

Von felt humiliated at that point, but he knew in his heart that the broad was right. He at least had to give himself a chance. So he sucked-up his pride and mumbled with fear in his voice.

"Ple- please don't kill me."

"Is that the best you can do? You damn sho' ain't gon' win no oscar's wit' that performance, now come again."

"Please don't kill me! Please don't!"

"Now that's much better... I'll tell you what I'ma do. I'll consider your plea, depending on the effectiveness of your answers to my questions. Bet?"

"B-bet." Von stated uneasily.

"Now, is this assassination attempt on my husband personal, or are you fulfilling a contract?"

"Fullfilling a contract." Answered Von.

"For who?"

"A dude name Lane"

"How much?"

Von hesitated for a moment because he figured this might turn into an opportunity. He would go up on the price in hopes of her making a sweeter offer for Lane, then in turn, Lane would triple the ticket for her and her husband. And he would still come out on top after he murdered them both.

"A hundred thousand." He answered.

"A hundred thousand, is that all?" Sheila asked in a sarcastic tone.

"Ye- yeah, that's what he said."

"Okay, this is what I'm gonna do. I'ma ask you one more question, and if I feel that you gave me a genuinely honest answer, you win. But, if I feel that you are lying to me again, you lose…. Now, let's say I gave you two-hundred thousand to reverse that contract and eliminate Lane. Would you be a man of your word and fulfill the contract and go your separate way afterwards? Or would you negotiate a better offer with Lane, then in turn, try to assassinate me and my husband?"

Von's mind was goin' a hundred miles a minute. He felt that it was a trick question. A game of psychology that she was running. He remembered a similar tactic used by his guidance counselor when he was in juvenile detention for assault with a knife on a classmate in junior high. The counselor would always ask his group if they were remorseful or not. And everytime they would all express how remorseful they were, they would all seem to be punished indirectly. But when they started answering with

"No, not really because the guy deserved it." They would seem to get rewarded.

"This bitch think she slick." He thought to himself. *"I know how this shit go."*

Von cleared his throat, then answered with a sincere tone as he pretended to feel defeated.

"Ay yo shorty, I'ma keep it one hundred with you. At first, I woulda' renegotiated the numbers with dude and came back to peel yall caps. But being that you is thorough as you is, I'd have to honor your contract on the up and up and split dat nigga's wig instead."

Sheila paused for a long fifteen seconds after hearing his statement, then flatly stated,

"You lose" –Boh! …The 380 bullet entered his skull and exited thru his left eye. He dropped like a sack of potatoes and twitched for a few seconds before he was officially lifeless…

Ray Ray quickly cut off the running water from the shower when he thought he heard a gunshot. He didn't bother to dry off completely, he dabbed the thick bath towel over his eyes a few times then wrapped it around his waist. He eased out of the bathroom as if somebody else was in the house that he didn't want to hear him. He instantly felt better when he secured the 44 bulldog and crept toward the front door.

"What the fuck." He mumbled as he cocked the weapon and walked barefoot over the carpeted floor. He didn't have a peephole, so he had to quickly resort to peeking from the blind of the closest window to the door… At first he thought his eyes were deceiving him, but they weren't. It was really her. Ray Ray snatched the door open in a hurry, and Sheila didn't waste any time jumping into his arms.

"Oh baby I missed you so much." Sheila whispered over and over between aggressive kisses.

"Me too baby, me too," answered Ray Ray as he held her tight. A few moments later, Sheila suddenly stopped all movement, then whispered.

"Come with me."

Ray Ray quickly went and slipped on some sweatpants, a t-shirt, and Timberland boots with no socks. He followed Sheila outside to where she had slumped Von, then listened to her explain what happened. Ray Ray dragged Von's body to the back of the house, then tossed an old mattress from the alley over it. After that, he took Sheila by the hand and led her back inside the house. Then made a mental note too himself that Lane was definitely on his shit list. Ray Ray fixed himself a shot of Hennessy, and Sheila a glass of Moscato.

After he downed the shot, he cleared his throat and attempted to tell her how sorry he was about all that he'd put her through. But Sheila cut his words off mid-sentence and spoke up.

"Ray Ray, you don't have nothing to be sorry about baby. I'm the one who's sorry. Sorry for not waking up a long time ago. Let's just say I've finally learned the limitations of kindness. And from now on, nothing will ever change the way I feel about you. My love for you is eternal. And the only way I will ever leave your side, is death. We said 'til death do us part, remember?"

"Yeah, we did." Ray Ray answered in a low gasp.... Sheila looked away momentarily, then locked eyes with him again.

"Ray Ray, at first I was a virgin to it. But, you allowed me to taste it when you came into my life."

"Ta- Taste what Sheila?" He asked confused with

wrinkled brows.

She smiled in a similar fashion of a little girl receiving her first doll, then answered.

"The thrill of victory baby... And now I understand why you always face problems so aggressively." A blank expression appeared on her face before she continued.

"Because aggression is sometimes the only element that gets your point across effectively."

Ray Ray was more than grateful for his woman to be on the same accord with him, but he could clearly see that she was out of sync with her normal character. On the surface, she seemed like your ordinary Sheila. But you had to know Sheila to recognize the missing element in her.

"Ray Ray, the world makes way for the man who knows where he's goin. I know where you're goin' baby, and I'll be right by your side when we get there. Baby you are my catalyst... Without you, I don't bloom."

Ray Ray knew the term *"Temporary Insanity'* all too well. And the more she talked, the more he realized it was standing right in front of him in the form of his wife.

He was now fully aware of what was goin' on. The pressure had been building inside of Sheila for the longest. And he'd pin-pointed the root of her change. The homicide, the incarceration, the kidnapping of her children, and now a new baby by a hoe. That was the breaking point for her. The straw that broke the camel's back. And the evidence of it was clearly reeking from her demeanor. But despite what was taking place, he knew he had a damn good woman, and she was worth her weight in gold. But somewhere in her psyche was a tremendous fury, and she had no intentions on allowing that emotion to go unfulfilled.

Sheila focused on Ray Ray with a sensuous glare, then unexpectedly pulled herself closer to him, slipping her tongue deep in his mouth. Her breathing became heavy as her tongue swam deeper. Ray Ray aggressively caressed her body, then went straight for the zipper on her lowrider jeans. She gladly helped him get them unfastened as quickly as possible, as her insatiable desire for him grew faster by the seconds.

They both assisted one another in taking off pieces of their clothes as they walked and fondled each other in route to the bedroom. They were completely naked by the time they made it to the bedroom. Ray Ray kissed around her ears and neck, then licked and sucked on her protruding nipples. He gave each breast equal time, then kissed his way down her cinnamon skin to her sweet moist flesh. Sheila moaned and slid forward forming a deep arch in the small of her back the moment his tongue flapped across her aching clitoris.

He wrapped his lips around her clit and sucked it gently, then teased it with the tip of his tongue as Sheila squirmed and tried to run from the pleasure. Ray Ray gripped her soft ass-cheeks and made his tongue flicker over her love button until she just couldn't take it anymore. She came fast and hard, and Ray Ray was reluctant to give her time to fully recuperate from the huge orgasm... He rolled her over, then spreaded her ass-cheeks and inserted a thumb in her asshole. Sheila moaned and pushed herself into him as he continued to push his thumb deeper inside her. She was more than ready to be penetrated, and she badly wanted to feel him inside her. She leaned forward, reached back, getting a firm grip on his throbbing pole, then eagerly guided it up to her warm opening. Ray Ray didn't hesitate to thrust forward.

"Ungh!..SS ooh Bay-bee." Sheila grunted as he gripped her hips and pumped her hole slow, then fast.

He watched as his hard flesh stretched her open, then suddenly glisten into a shiny dark-brown pole from being coated with her continuous flow of juices. Sheila's breasts bounced with every stroke, and she closed her eyes and let out soft moans as he aggressively dug into her. After ten minutes of fucking her doggystyle, he laid on his back and let Sheila ride him... She straddled herself on him facing his feet, then slowly began to grind on his manhood in a steady, slow rhythm.

Ray Ray loved the way she gyrated her hips and made her phat ass bounce up and down on him in strip-dancer fashion. She moved like a slinky, and when she adjusted her double-jointed legs and gripped his ankles, he entered a world that only Sheila could take him too.

His dick bounced, leaned, and twirled around inside her, touching everything that was biologically inside of her pussy. She moved the way a Jamaican woman moved on the dance floor as she whined the way R-Kelly would ask her too in a song. All Ray Ray could do was lean his head back and close his eyes, 'cause like always, Sheila had a gangsta on the ropes... He was trying his damnest to hold back because it felt so good. But the combination of her movements, dirty talk, and whimpering, had him holding on for dear life.

"I wanna cum baby, make me cum baby. Ssmm, I need you to cum with me Ray Ray. Don't hold back." Sheila's pace picked up tremendously, and their pulsating rhythms complimented each other as Ray Ray found himself about to explode.

Sheila came seconds before him, and just as he was

about to bust, she leaped up off of him and quickly slid his pipe in her mouth. She bobbed her head in a fast-paced up and down motion as she swallowed as much of him as she could...

"Mmm." She moaned as Ray Ray's toes curled and his load suddenly exploded in her mouth.

Sheila continued to lick and suck him 'til his convulsions completely stopped. Then she looked up at him seductively and mouthed,

"I love you baby, and I always will."... They took a bath together, then talked until they fell asleep.

CHAPTER 25

Shortly after Sheila awoke the next morning, weariness had her firmly in its grip. She'd initially arisen in good spirits, but fatigue plainly showed on her face after noticing the piece of paper beside the bed on the nightstand.

As Ray Ray slept, she'd read Syann's bail information, and it only ignited the anger that already festered in her for Syann. Sheila took a shower then quietly got dressed. She slid on a pair of black Burberry jeans, a black button-up sleeveless Burberry shirt, along with a casual pair of black Chanel boots with a three-inch heel. Then she accentuated her attire with a short black leather jacket, a scarf, and a dark pair of Chanel shades... After looking herself over in the mirror and satisfied with her appearance, she eased out quietly without waking Ray Ray.

Sheila made it to the Wayne County Jail in thirty-five minutes. She looked herself over once more, then thought to herself,

"This should be a cinch."

She strolled through the front door and put her fake I.D. to work.

"May I help you?" asked a heavyset white officer at the front desk who looked like he spent the bulk of his paycheck at Dunkin Donuts and neglected his dental responsibilities.

"Yes you may." Answered Sheila politely.

"I'm here to bail out a Syann Ross."

"Sy-ann Ross, Ross, Ross," mumbled the officer as he thumbed through a thick book where inmates are logged in at.

"Ah, here we go right here." He said as he read her status.

"Fleeing and eluding capture. I see she's got a little rabbit in her huh? Ha, Ha."

Sheila gave a half-hearted smile at the officer's sarcastic comment, then waited impatiently as he pussy-footed around and tried to make small-talk through the entire process.

"Finally!" she thought to herself after she paid the bail and waited in the car.

Sheila pulled out the 380 pistol and re-checked the firing mechanisms again. She wanted to make sure there were no mishaps once she started firing rounds into Syann's body. She couldn't wait to get it done, because she felt that Syann had put her husband through too much already. She turned on the radio while she waited, and the smooth tunes of Heather Headley's 'In My Mind' only reminded her of the way she felt about her husband.

"In my mind, I'll always be his lady. In my mind, I'll always be his girl."

She gently tapped the steering wheel as she sung along with the words...

"Ross! Pack it up!" yelled the dep. Syann leaped to her feet then dumped a couple cigarettes out from the generic pack she held, then handed the rest of the pack to a twenty-one-year-old chick name Laqueeda.

"Yall take it easy girl. I'll call yo baby-daddy and tell'em what yo' bond is soon as I step out this bitch, okay."

"Okay girl, I appreciate it. You hold it down out there a'ight."

"Fasho' girl. I'll holla." Said Syann as she exited the cell…

After going through the process of signing a couple forms and dressing out, Syann was ready to go. And even though she'd only been incarcerated for less than 24 hours, she was ready to take a hot bath, and more than ready to eat some real food followed by a few stiff lines of cocaine.

"I'ma put on some sexy-ass shit tonight and convince Ray Ray to fuck the shit outta me like he did the last time… Damn I wish he would leave his wife and be my man. Dat nigga just don't know how good I would be to him. It's time for me to stop bullshitten and make him mine. I gotta step my game up. Me, him, and our son together. That would definitely make my life complete. I'm goin' for it." Syann concluded her thoughts and smiled as she sashayed toward the front door.…

When Ray Ray awoke, he somehow wasn't surprised to find Sheila out of bed before him. Even though he'd been getting up before her for years, she put it on him last night so he figured she'd beat him up this morning. He strolled to the bathroom and took a piss that seemed to take forever to stop flowing. Then he washed his hands and walked to the kitchen in search of Sheila. He cased the rest of the house looking for her when he saw that she wasn't in the kitchen, then went back to the bedroom and sat on the bed…

"She must've went to the store." He thought to himself.

He tried not to get too agitated about it, but with all the heat that was on them, he knew that stores were relatively dangerous because most of them had customer surveillance cameras.

As he sat there wondering which store she could've gone too, his heart suddenly skipped a beat and he anxiously began searching for the piece of paper with Syann's bail information on it....

After three minutes of meticulous searching, he knew what had happened to it and now knew where Sheila went... He hurriedly put on some clothes, then snatched the keys off the dresser that he'd took off Von's body.

He rushed to the cutlass, then skidded off wildly seconds later headed for the county hoping he wasn't too late.

As Syann stepped out the front door into the late September breeze, she inhaled the fresh air and was thankful for it in place of the stale air that circulated through the crampy cellblocks... She anxiously scanned the area looking for any familiar faces but surprisingly she saw none.

She trudged down a few steps, still scanning the area while Sheila focused on her intently. Sheila slipped her pistol-gripped hand into the right pocket of her jacket, then climbed from the car and strolled toward Syann with a blank expression. Syann didn't seem to notice Sheila's approach, but just as they locked eyes with each other,

"Hey! Hey! Hey!" yelled the two desk officers who stormed through the front door behind Syann...

Syann was startled, and briskly turned around to see what all their hostility was about. One of the men held a piece of paper in hand, while the other one dangled a pair of handcuffs in front of her.

"Turn around and place your hands behind your back."

Demanded the officer with the cuffs.

"What the fuck is goin' on? I just made bond." Syann scowled in a confused tone.

"You see this?" asked the officer with the document in his hand as he pointed to the letters D.T.S in the left-hand corner.

"Yeah, what about it?" asked Syann suspiciously.

"Well, it means 'Detain Suspect.' And what that means sweetheart is, the feds have a detainer on you for further investigation of some sort. And we are not supposed to release you until they say so. You'll have another bond hearing soon, so don't get discouraged, you're gonna be alright."

"How in the fuck I'ma be alright! Huh! I got a muthafuckin child I gotta get to!" Syann nutted up and became a little resistant as they cuffed her and placed her back in custody.

As she turned to walk back in the station, her eyes met with Sheila's again, and she suddenly got the feeling that something wasn't right about the attractive woman with the dark shades. Yet in all actuality, she still didn't realize how close she came to biting the dust.

"Damn" mumbled Sheila as she cursed herself for letting a golden opportunity pass. She felt that she should've gunned all three of them down instead of letting Syann get away. She stood there in the middle of the street fuming as Syann and the two officers disappeared through the doors.

She snapped out of her daze a few moments later when Ray Ray pulled up and came to a screeching halt. He exited the car and approached her in a few short strides. He looked her over and let her distraught expression tell the story.

He decided to touch on the subject briefly, then leave it alone.

"Baby, if you woulda' done what you came to do, it would'na solved nothin. The fact is, I still got a child by her. And whether she dead or alive, I'm still gon' have a child by her. So shake that shit off baby and help me figure out our next move. 'Cause we inn over our heads already, and now ain't the time to fall apart. Come on, let's go."

He took her hand and led her to the Toyota she drove. They pulled off leaving Von's cutlass abandoned, parked across the street from the county.

Fifteen minutes later, Ray Ray coasted to a slow stop in front of Oeekwa's house as she stood there with little Ray waiting for his arrival. Ray Ray got out the car and instinctively eyed the entire length of the block until he made it to where she stood.

"Hey Ray Ray. Syann just called and told me what happened with her bail situation, so I guess all we can do is just wait 'til we hear something.

Lil Ray's been asking about you every hour on the hour. *"When my daddy comin' back when my daddy comin' back.* Drivin me crazy." She mocked.

"So I got all his stuff packed for you, and here's the vase with Smo-..." She stopped in mid-sentence and searched her mind for a more subtle delivery. She came up with none, so she just gently handed it to him and let the empathy she wanted to express radiate from her hazel brown eyes. She was almost as pretty as Syann. And as Ray Ray stood there appreciating her humbleness, he thought to himself,

"All the bitches in her family must be fine." He handed her a stack of bills in the amount of five-thousand dollars. Thanked her, then left with Sheila and lil Ray....

As they drove back to the safe-house, Sheila starred at the little man intently. She wanted to find a reason to hate him as much as she hated his mother, but she couldn't. Because he was as innocent as the glare in his big brown eyes. And his overwhelming resemblance to Ray Ray wouldn't allow her to hate nothing about his precious existence.

After she analyzed him and formed a silent truce in her mind with him, she casually held out her hand.

"Hi sweetheart. My name is Sheila, and it's so nice to meet you." She noted with a smile. Lil Ray seemed a bit shy, and he hesitated for a moment. But when his mind conveyed to him that Sheila wasn't a threat, he extended his tiny hand out, placing it into hers.

Ray Ray stole a quick glance and didn't say a word. He gave a light smile and felt good about their acquaintance, because that was exactly what he wanted. This was one-half of the only things he cared about in the world, and he needed nothing less than a willing alliance from all parties.

After they made it back to the safe-house, Ray Ray stopped abruptly when they approached the front door. He suddenly moved slowly and motioned for Sheila to stand back. He pulled out the 44, then quickly pushed the already cracked door all the way open.

He aimed the gun in front of him as he meticulously stepped through the ransacked house. He carefully searched every room before informing Sheila that it was alright to enter, then wondered to himself who in the hell had done this. He noticed that the few guns he had there were gone, along with the eleven-thousand dollars he had sitting on the dresser. He knew he didn't have time to play any guessing games, so he glanced around momentarily with his mind in 'Think fast mode, then instructed Sheila to take lil Ray and wait outside in the car.

He ran out back and dragged Von's body inside, then he thoroughly wiped the house clean of fingerprints. He grabbed a bottle of ammonia and emptied the entire bottle over the few pieces of furniture that was there and all over the carpeted floor...

Just as he was about to spark the lighter, he noticed a brown stuffed teddy-bear about the size of a three-year-old sitting on the living room floor with a note attached to it. Ray Ray skeptically glanced around the house once more, then read the note.

Ray Ray, in my profession, it is always wise for men like myself to be informed, alert, and to grow eyes in the back of my head. Therefore, I'm granted the luxury of seeing further than most. Along with the ability to hear a mouse piss on cotton if need be... I want you to know that I'm extremely upset about the recent string of robberies that's taken place with some of my most profitable business associates. People like Lane, Tree-lo, Mike, and Tee, just to name a few. Well, it's come to the point that I'm all out of warnings with you Ray Ray. So this short notation is basically to inform you that I consider you as nothing less than the enemy. And I've officially declared an all-out war against you. Ray Ray your father was truly indeed a friend. But, his name no longer protects you from the wrath that I bring down on those whom I feel disrespect me. But, I was still decent enough to hold your name in high regard. I complimented your underworld status by placing a one-million-dollar price on your head. Mainly because of your consistency. But mostly because of your ambition and the fact that you stole a lot of my currency. I'm sure you've already realized you weren't ready for this level of the game. But just think of it like this. It was fun while it lasted, but all good things must come to an end... Oh, and by the way, I told you Deo was just a teddy-bear. The eyes never lie amigo."

Ray Ray balled up the letter, then slowly picked up the teddy-bear, puzzled about Mr. Alverez's last statement... After five brief seconds of looking the bear over, he startlingly dropped it and took a step back. He now understood what Mr. Alverez meant by *"The eyes never lie,"* because it was clear to see that the light-colored human eyes that were stitched into the sockets of where the teddy-bear's eyes use to be, belonged to none other than Deo.

"Shrewd mu-tha-fucka." Ray Ray mumbled to himself as he stood there focusing on the psychotic demonstration that clearly displayed the level of discipline Mr. Alverez had for his organization. Ray Ray knew Mr. Alverez always took his threats seriously and would do everything in his power to have his contract fulfilled. But war was in Ray Ray's blood, and he welcomed the drama that was soon to come. He just hoped that he wouldn't be apprehended by authorities by the time he went to pay Mr. Alverez a visit.

He shrugged it off, then sparked the lighter to life... He set the house ablaze, then pulled off in the car with Sheila and his son, headed for the Metro Airport.....

CHAPTER 26

3 days later.

As Ray Ray, Sheila, and lil Ray stepped through the front door of Yvonne's house in L.A, Myonly and Love rushed into their arms and expressed how much they missed them. They were ecstatic and overjoyed and didn't calm down for another thirty minutes.

After all the commotion had finally settled down, Ray Ray sat them down and introduced them to their brother. They didn't have half as many questions as he thought they would, but they were rather excited about lil Ray, and accepted him with open arms.

While the children played x-box games and Sheila pecked on her laptop, Ray Ray spoke in a slow, measured tone when he asked Yvonne if he could speak with her in private for a minute...

She agreed, then he reluctantly stepped off into the kitchen with her.

Ray Ray looked down at the small crystal vase in his hands, then cleared his throat and gave a brief explanation.

"Yvonne, first of all, this shit is fuckin' me up right now to have to tell you this. But, I'm gon' spare myself the agony and try to spit it out as quickly as possible... This belongs to you." He handed her the vase then continued.

"Smoke told me that if anything ever happened to him,

he wanted to be cre-, he requested to be cre-," he paused when his stammered words wouldn't come out right, then tried to continue.

"Cremated when he- left, so-." Yvonne held up a hand to relieve him of the difficult duty of telling a mother her only son was deceased.

She didn't respond the way he anticipated her too. She just stood there in a subtle manner and sniffed a few times as the single tear crept down her aged, attractive dark face. She took a deep breath in an effort to maintain her composure, then quietly strolled to the bathroom with her hand to her chest and her head hung low. Yvonne had already been aware of what happened because she'd actually felt it in her gut for a week or so. Her motherly instincts told her that her son was no longer among the living. The game was over. And the only thing that she'd been waiting for thus far was confirmation... And unfortunately, it finally came.

****

Boom!

"Dammit this is not a fuckin game!" yelled Special Agent Barker as he slammed his fist against the steel table in the interrogation room.... Syann cringed at his tantrum but still remained silent as he carried on.

"You naïve bitches really puzzle me. You let these low life's get in your head, toss around a little cash, skeet up in you at random, and you play the fool until you're all used up. I got a dead informant, a dead special agent, and a bunch of other dead individuals that bastard-friend of yours is responsible for. Why would you protect a mutherfucker like that? He's a cold ruthless sonuvabitch.

And mark my words lady, we will get his ass with you or without you. And as of this point, you've only got 24 hours to make up your mind on helping yourself. 'Cause after that, I'm charging you with the two kilos of cocaine that we found by the informant, and conspiracy to the murder of a federal informant. And don't get cute and think you can beat it, 'cause from the information we have from the wiretaps alone, it will make crazy glue look watered down. This shit will stick to your ass better than a mouse on a sticky trap...better yet, a fuckin tattoo!!" He stormed toward the door with built-up saliva in the corners of his mouth, then angrily turned around before walking out.

"24 hours beautiful!" he shouted sarcastically as he attempted to slam the door behind him.

"Wait!" yelled Syann, stopping him in motion.

"What is it. 'Cause like I said, I don't have time for games." He noted snobbishly.

Syann instinctively dropped her head in a saddened manner, with her mouth formed tightly as if she was full of regret. She was handcuffed to the front instead of the back, and her deep dimples combined with her wavy ponytail gave her an innocent, yet exotic look. She slowly raised her head and made eye contact with agent Barker before she spoke up.

"I- I just wanted to say, I didn't have it easy growin up. And because of my upbringing, I truly did end up bringing some unpleasant issues with me into my adulthood. But, is it really my fault that I was dealt a bad hand? If I had a choice in the matter I would've been a rich preppy Harvard student who had doctors for parents and didn't give up my virginity until I was at least twenty-five."

"So what are you saying? You say all that to say what?" Agent Barker asked with a hint of agitation still in his voice.

"I say all that to say, in a sense, you were right about bitches like me. Ya see, I've been fuckin' with cruddy niggas all my life, and I mean aallll my life. My first date, cruddy nigga. My first kiss, cruddy nigga. My first dick, cruddy nigga. And my first orgasm, cruddy nigga... And sittin' in here listening to the things you said to me, finally shed some light on my situation. It's really simple when you look at it... As simple as eagles don't hang with chickens 'cause chickens can't fly. Birds of a feather flock together. I fuck wit' cruddy niggas 'cause I'm a cruddy bitch! And today I not only learned something about myself, I learned something about you.

"I learned that use'a cruddy cracker. I know because my pussy aaallllwaays get wet for cruddy muthafuckas. Now talk some more of that humiliating shit that you was talkin' a minute ago, 'cause I can cum real hard when you talk like that." Syann licked her tongue out seductively at his back as the door slammed hard behind him. She laughed heartily to herself because she knew she was extremely talented at getting under a man's skin whenever she chose to. She was considered a natural at the art of seduction, and it excited her more than sex or money whenever she put it to use.

Tears poured from Ebony's eyes as she stood beside her car on the shoulder of the 91 freeway with her cellphone pressed to her ear.

While Yvonne's phone rung, Ebony reflected on all the terrible things that took place in her life since she met Smoke. She'd became fed up with running from a fight that she felt wasn't hers, and it didn't surprise her when she gave the state trooper her real name after the traffic stop.

She found herself on the side of the freeway surrounded by law enforcement from three different agencies within a matter of minutes. And once the FBI commander informed her of Smoke's death, she found it hard to hold herself together.

"Hello." Yvonne finally answered the phone.

"Hey Yvonne, this is Eb, what's up?"

"Hey Eb! We was worried sick about you, where are you?"

"Um, I- I'm about a hour away, I just needed to clear my head and sort some things out."

"Girl I understand. So, are you coming back?"

Ebony paused as she tried to get her sniveling under control, then answered.

"Yeah, I'll be back."

"When?"

"Maybe in a couple of hours."

"Okay, I'll see you then."

"Uh- wai- Yvonne?"

"Yeah, I'm still here."

"Uh, are the babies alright?"

"Yeah, the babies are fine."

"How about Sheila and Ray Ray?"

"Yeah, they're here and they're fine too."

"Uh, so what's been going on since I've been gone?"

Yvonne was about to answer her, then suddenly paused when she began to process the entire situation through her mind. She noticed how extremely upset Ebony sounded, and something just didn't feel right.

Yvonne's mind was working overtime, and it was when she thought about the last peculiar detail, that she finally put the puzzle together in her mind… Ebony never asked about Smoke's whereabouts because she already knew. And her constant stammering and odd line of questioning only meant one thing to Yvonne, Ebony was trying to keep her on the phone until the police made it to her house.

Ebony had given up their location… Yvonne quickly shut the phone off, then ran in the living room and informed Ray Ray and Sheila.

Ray Ray signaled for everybody to stay put, then dashed out the back door… In a quick sprint and two small leaps, he was on the next block headed toward the corner. When he got there, he quickly dipped back when he saw the red Impala parked with three people inside. He quickly scanned the area for police before his eyes fell back upon the Impala. He couldn't make out who they were, but from their cunning movements and constant peeps out the window, they were definitely gangbangers about to put in work.

Ray Ray noticed that they were looking in the direction of Yvonne's house, so he intuitively ran back to the house and decided to see whether he was trippin' or not. He walked out the front door and casually climbed in Yvonne's green Explorer. When he backed out of the driveway, he quickly looked in the direction of the Impala and noticed the hydraulics bounce it to it's original height… He abruptly stopped the truck halfway down the driveway, then got out and went back inside…

"Hold up blood!" said Damon curtly as he watched Ray Ray run back into the house.

"Wait until everybody in the truck, then roll up on it so we can blast everybody in that bitch… babies and all." The other blood members laughed in sinister tones as they passed the blunt back and forth...

"Ray Ray what's goin' on... You know the police will be here any minute. We gotta' get the hell outta' here!" Sheila protested.

"Yeah Ray Ray, she's right." Added Yvonne emphatically.

"Mommy I'm scared." Whined Myonly as she listened to the panicky tones in the grown-ups voices.

"Everybody just chill a'ight. We gon' be alright!" Ray Ray had to tell a quick lie just to keep everybody from panicking any worse than they already were.

He pulled Sheila into the bedroom and whispered a set of instructions in her ear, then he anxiously searched through Rob's dresser-drawer looking for anything that might assist him in beating the odds.

After a few minutes of searching, he ran across a bunch of blue and red bandanas that were tightly tied together. Rob kept most of the bandanas tied together as a symbol of peace, and he would always toss them into his audience after a lecture in hopes that they would carry on the message and keep the peace-treaty alive.... Ray Ray's mind went in overdrive as he snatched a set from the drawer, then tucked Sheila's 380 in his waist and ran out of the room. He gave Sheila a quick glance of affection, then grabbed Rob's BMX titanium mountain bike that he used for exercise purposes and headed out the door....

Tires screeched and smoked as a slew of police cars swerved through traffic at high speeds headed to Yvonne's address in a hurry. The dispatcher consistently relayed codes, commands, and status-checks the whole time. And angry motorist's pulled over as the aggressive convoy bullied their way through the heavy traffic....

After Sheila placed seatbelts on all the children, she slowly pulled the truck out of the driveway...

Click-Clack! Click-Clack! - Click! Damon and his boys sleekly pulled the red bandanas over their faces after fully loading all of their weapons. They waited eagerly as the truck drove slowly in their direction.

"Remember what I said yall. Don't leave nothing breathin." Damon reminded his cronies as he gripped the Mp-5 machine gun tightly....

Just as Sheila made it to the corner, a burgundy Crown Victoria came sliding to a screeching halt, blocking their path with guns drew, barking orders.... A split second later, two L.A.P.D police cars left fresh skidmarks in the street as they also slid to a wild stop taking aim on the SUV.

As the two detectives in the burgundy Crown Vic continuously yelled for Sheila and Yvonne to show their hands and step out of the vehicle, they never noticed the man with the red bandana pulled over his face, roll up beside them on the mountain bike. "Boh! Boh! Boh! Boh! Boh!"

After giving both of the white detective's face shots, he leaped off the bike and sprinted over to the red Impala.

"Yo blood, them pigs tryna' ride on us!" he yelled in the window of the impala, then stooped low beside the car and let off more shots at the police.

Damon and the other two gang members instantly jumped out the car and open-fired relentlessly with the high-powered weapons they carried.

"Derrrr! Derrrr! Cac! Cac! Cac! Boh! Boh! Boh! Derrr! Derrr!" bullets riddled the four police cars and overkilled the two detectives that were already dead.

More police approached the scene and officers didn't

hesitate to join in on the fierce gun-battle that already claimed three of their own and had others scrambling for cover.

Sheila threw the truck in reverse and hurriedly backed away from the heated firefight, but one of the warring bloods noticed the truck backing away in his peripheral and open-fired in her direction.

Sheila and the kids screamed as the truck took a few hits, but she continued to hold it steady 'til she made it out of his line of fire.... "Boh!" The blood member dropped as the single bullet tore through the back of his head and lodged three inches from his left temple. Ray Ray picked up his machine gun afterwards and open-fired on the police again...

Damon and the remaining blood-member noticed their partner drop, but the battle was so intense that they thought it came from one of the police..... Five minutes later, it seemed as if the entire force was on the scene. Damon and his partner crouched uncomfortably behind the shredded Impala, angry because during the shootout, they never noticed the stray blood-member slip away and leave them there to continue the battle alone. Two helicopters continuously hovered low above the scene... One of them was the news, and the other was L.A.P.D...

As the swat team converged around the car, Damon angrily spit a glob of blood from the glass-cut on his lip, then looked at his homie with desperation in his eyes.

"Fuck it homie, let's give these bitches what they want."

They shook hands and threw up their set. Then in one swift motion, they both spent into plain view with their weapons spitting rapid fire...

The swat team briefly took cover, then let their three sharp shooters take aim with the high-powered assault rifles. Two of them kneeled on one knee, while the third one lay flat on the ground with his weapon rested on a small tripod…

Damon and his partner refused to let up, and as they strived to kill anything in their path, the professional assassins who meticulously peered through the high-powered scopes, simultaneously squoze off in three-second bursts. "Pow! Pow!…Pow!" Damon's body twisted and contorted as the big slugs tore through his flesh like a hot knife through butter.

He watched as the top of his friend's head came off as if he wore a toupee all along. He was deceased before he hit the ground.

Damon finally dropped flat on his back from the violent assault, and as his body lay twisted like a discarded ragdoll… His adrenaline-filled nerves caused his body to jerk a few times before he finally became forever relaxed.

The FBI commander gave strict orders to comb every inch of the area in search of Ray Ray, Sheila, and the third blood member… which was also Ray Ray.

They found Yvonne's Explorer parked and abandoned on a side street seven blocks away, then continued the search for five hours straight… to no avail.

"Still at large. I repeat, the suspects are still at large," said the dispatcher.

Agent Burns waited patiently until everyone was seated in the twenty chairs that occupied the debriefing room on the fifth floor of the federal building in Downtown Detroit.

He shuffled a small stack of papers in his hands and cleared his throat before speaking.

"Okay listen up people. I'm sure by now most of you are already familiar with the Raynard Thompson case."

A few unenthused *"yeah's,"* *grunts,* and *"mmhmm,'s"* came forward as an answer to his statement.

"Yeah...Yeah, I feel the same way but don't get discouraged, because you' all know, we always get our man. Now, I just wanted to inform you'all that we have new information that gives us more of a logical explanation on his wife's successful escape from Coldwater Michigan's maximum security female prison. We believe that a female correctional officer by the name of Lakeda McPherson, who works at the facility, gave Ray Ray a blueprint of the joint and aided him in his efforts in exchange for money.

On the day of the escape, Lakeda called in sick, and claimed that a black correctional officer by the name of Mr. Darrell Robinson was going to fill in for her. But once he was logged into the roster book, he never showed up. We recently questioned him and we think his absence may have been legit. He says he agreed to fill in for her but had a last-minute change of plans because his eight-year-old son became ill. Which is when he called and informed her that he wouldn't be able to make it. She agreed and they hung up... Now, when we checked into his claims, St. John's hospital verifies the fact that the child was indeed brought into emergency that night.

But, when we questioned her, she says he never called back. And as far as she knew, he was going to fill in for her like he agreed too. Which, in turn points the finger at him because number one, his name is on the roster as her replacement. And number two, although he denies ever calling in that night to clarify it, the duty Lt. says that a man definitely called in claiming to be Mr. Robinson and logged into the books as the replacement scheduled to show up.

But, who shows up instead! Our main man Ray Ray. And that's when it all goes down. Now Mr. Robinson and Lakeda have both been suspended pending further investigation. And we've been keeping a close watch on both of them, especially Lakeda because we honestly feel that she's our perpetrator. She has no serious criminal record, but ever since she's been a correctional officer, she's been under investigation several times by her administration for different things like bringing in drugs, sex toys, and other miscellaneous items to accommodate some of the female prisoners. She was also once accused of planning an escape for a wealthy white girl who'd killed her husband for gawking at another woman. But Ms. Lily ended up getting cold feet about it and backed out. Then ratted Lakeda out to her superior officers. But of course, Lakeda denied it, and ended up getting fully reinstated after the investigation.

At first we were kind of puzzled as to how she kept getting around the system without ever getting completely fired or reprimanded. Then it all made sense when we found out who her uncle is. He's actually the governor of Michigan. Governor Harold McPherson to be more specific. She's his youngest neice, 28 years old, and they are extremely close. So with that being said, I'm sure I don't have to remind you' all of the delicate nature of this case. So make sure we cross all our t's and dot all our I's during this investigation, understood? Your dismissed."

One month later... As Ray Ray sat on the edge of his bed and talked on his cell phone, he glanced at the 6 p.m. Detroit breaking news report. They were discussing a large-scale cocaine bust that produced 800 kilos of good quality coke and 3.2 mil in cash. Three people were arrested in the bust, and more indictments are expected to be served. Ray Ray smirked to himself because he knew that the only reason they were broadcasting every large bust on the tv lately, was because election time was coming up soon. He wrote down some valuable information about Mr. Alverez that he received from the governor's niece Lakeda, then thanked her and told her they'd be intouch. Ray Ray reflected on how Mr. Alverez was the only reason he didn't utilize the many passports he had, and just leave the country again, never to be heard from again... He had it all, a beautiful wife who was loyal to his every desire. Millions of tax-free dollars. And three of the most precious children a person could ever wish for. But despite his clear path to a clean exit, a full-scale war had been waged against him. And he wasn't the type of man that ran from wars, he embraced them.

To go away, in his mind would be running from a fight. Similar to a fearful dog with his tail curled between his legs as his opponent bit chunks of flesh from his scouring body. It would be like waving a white flag. A cowardice move that wouldn't allow him to get a wink of sleep at night. He was a rebel with a 'cause and had no regard for those who didn't understand him.

The self-centered pride that's harbored deep within his psyche, wouldn't allow him to take the prize and go. Instead, he would ignore the consequences of possibly being annihilated, and losing all that he lived for in the name of facing his enemies. Ray Ray's life was clearly not a movie, but in similarity to one of his favorite movies, he truly understood why Robert Deneiro went back to finish what fate had started. It was the calling of something bigger than him, and it screamed to be unleashed... Ray

Ray was truly among *The Last Breed of Gangsta's,* and nine times out of ten, he would ultimately die one.

And even though Sheila's 'temporary insanity situation' had faded from her character, she still chose to remain near her man until he would either succumb from a collision with his enemies, or sit patiently in a rocking chair and tell his grandchildren how the hood almost took him under...

The stage was set and he continuously puffed on the Newport cigarette as he looked over the double-digit list of people who associated with Mr. Alverez. He drew a line through one of the names with a black ink-pen, then zipped his black hooded Nike-Flight jacket up over his Kevlar vest. He mashed the cigarette out, glanced at his watch, then grabbed the duffle-bag full of weapons and headed out the door.......

EPILOGUE

Although Ebony was more than willing to co'operate with authorities, she was still charged with Aiding and Abetting murderers, drug dealers, and fugitives.

She was sentenced to ten years in federal prison with the promise of a time-cut upon the capture of her co'conspirators....

Syann stayed true to the code of silence and ended up charged with the two kilos of powder cocaine they'd found and a few other trumped-up charges that also earned her a sentence of ten years in federal prison. They also tried to charge her with Sporty's murder, but his wiretaps actually saved her from the conviction....

Yvonne used some of Rob's political connections to clear her name from any speculations of wrongdoing, and picked up where Rob left off by joining a chapter of the NAACP in Detroit. She temporarily cut her ties with Ray Ray and Sheila and stayed diligent in her quest to clean up high-crime neighborhoods in most Metropolitan cities. She became the Assistant Director in a short period of time and led the coalition of a movement she sparked entitled, 'Operation Hood Driven.' Her intentions were to reach the residents of the hood and turn their negative purposes into positive ones. Her outlook on the matter was, instead of letting the hood drive you to kill a person, we should let the hood drive you into a predicament of saving a person mentally, physically, and economically. Ultimately preserving black life, starting from the womb.

Although Sheila was a fugitive, she still resorted back to some of her past business ventures. She briefly dabbled in residential real-estate, but her primary focus was building a franchise of Shelters for the poor and disenfranchised. And despite her gangstress edge, she was a savvy professional when it came to making a legal profit. And she truly wanted to leave her children a legacy they could be proud of…

As for Ray Ray, he is currently being heavily pursued by the FBI, ATF, DEA. Special Weapons And Tactics unit, (SWAT). And a few other law enforcement agencies…. Too this date, he still remains Hood Driven…

ACKNOWLEDGEMENTS

Whuddup doe world, here we go again, history in the making. Let's get it. First off, I gotta thank the creator for allowing me to keep this heat comin yall way, and opening doors that got the future lookin real bright. I'm feelin good about the material that's being pushed through Deep-Street Publications. It's everything that my supporters expect from me, and yall gotta know I thank yall wholeheartedly for every grain of support that yall been giving me from day one of my grind... especially the females, yall are phenomenal and I can't thank yall enough. Yall are the ones that got the Hood Driven series bangin' right now. And I definitely gotta thank all my gangsta's, thugs, homies, friends, family, and without a doubt my wife Shermane.   co-CEO of Deep-Street publications for riding with me through every struggle nomatter how difficult things got. And finding the mental and physical endurance to assist in making our dreams come true. I love you baby, you are the realest, thank you. And once again to all my supporters, creating street-lit is a beautiful feeling, and I'm excited about giving yall the real from a real perspective. Ray Hill from Don Diva Magazine, whuddup big homie, much love and respect for all of your assistance. Crystal Perkins, by way of mink magazine, the article you gave me was beautiful. Thank you my dear friend. I gotta thank all the radio networks and stores that showed me love. The D been holdin me down to the fullest, along with the rest of the mid-west, east-coast, and west-coast states that's been showin me love as well. I thank yall humbly. Whuddup Ms. Angel Flew, world renown author who just dropped two best-sellers, Behind closed doors, and Teenagers who tell it all. keep doin' yo thang my friend. Ronnika Harris, whuddup doe. Kedie, love you sis. Times truly are strange these days, stay focused and let's definitely keep campaigning about cleaning up Michigan State Police Corruption. It's rotten to the core over there, facts. Whuddup Shon, Shantae, Shontell, Selena, Daminya, Kim, Juanita Cooper. And all the book clubs that supported my projects, thank you much. To my two stepsons Shaquille and Poppi. Thanks for making my job fun. And representing yall-selves the way young men are supposed to. I love yall. To my brother Suge, and the rest of my brothers on lock in federal and state prisons, keep yall heads up warriors, a change is definitely gon' come. Whuddup Heem, and big dog Jermaine still holdin down that eastside. Diop. Welcome home Donald B. I have a million more people that I'd like to name, but it's all good 'cause I got all of yall in my heart. So, until we do it again, I promise to keep bringing that heat for yall. This literature thang runs deep in my blood. I was born to do it and love doin' it... R.I.P Demetrius Gray. R.I.P Raphael Rock Washington. Chris Crenshaw. Cosmo. And all the other fallen warriors who left us way too soon. You will be in our hearts forever. Holla atcha boy... I love you Priya Mack, forever and a day.

ABOUT THE AUTHOR:

Derek Mack, a-k-a D-Mack was raised by his grandmother on the eastside of Detroit Michigan. He is personally in tune with most of the harsh realities that jump from the pages of his crime novels and is certified as being True to the Game by those who played in his circle.

D-Mack is an avid reader and was inspired to pursue a writing career from authors such as, Iceberg Slim, Sister Souljah, Charles Avery Harris and many more. He is currently hard at work creating new material and has a real passion for the literary world. He say's that he is most at peace whenever he's writing stories, sharing his craft with those who enjoy genuine creativity.